PRAYERWORKS

PRAYERWORKS

Equipping the Church for action

11 10 09 08 07 06 05   7 6 5 4 3 2 1

First published 2005 by Spring Harvest Publishing Division and
Authentic Media, 9 Holdom Avenue, Bletchley, Milton Keynes, Bucks,
MK1 1QR, UK
and 129 Mobilization drive, Waynesboro, GA 30830-4575, USA
www.authenticmedia.co.uk

British Library Cataloguing in Publication Data
A catalogue record for this book is available from the British Library

ISBN 1-85078-631-3

Cover design by Sam Redwood
Print Management by Adare Carwin
Printed and Bound by J. H. Haynes & Co. Ltd., Sparkford

CONTENTS

PRAYERWORKS

AN INTRODUCTION

Dear Lord, the Great Healer, I kneel before you,
Since every perfect gift must come from you.
I pray, give skill to my hands, clear vision to my mind,
kindness and meekness to my heart.
Give me singleness of purpose, strength to lift up a part
Of the burden of my suffering fellow man,
And a true realisation of the privilege that is mine.
Take from my heart all guile and worldliness,
That with the simple faith of a child, I may rely on you.

From *A Simple Heart*, by Mother Teresa [1]

This is the prayer, written by Mother Teresa, that every Missionary of Charity says each day before ministering to the dying. It is the intimate prayer of those most actively involved in the pain of the real world. Every single morning these quiet heroes kneel before the 'Lord, the Great Healer' precisely because the ravages of sickness await their attention. In prayer, each missionary volunteers daily to 'lift up a part of the burden of my suffering fellow man', and somehow finds the strength to count such service a 'privilege'. Having surrendered before God 'all guile and worldliness', they plunge into the wretchedness of the very world they have renounced.

Such saints remind us that intimacy with God and involvement in his world are inseparably linked. Prayer is practical. They demonstrate a devotional life that propels us out from the cloisters of God's presence to fulfil his purposes tangibly in society. They remind us that – to coin the title of this book – prayer works not just as the primary means of *spiritual formation*, but also – surprisingly – as the primary agency of *social transformation* as well. As Dr Luke makes clear, the earliest Christians not only 'devoted themselves to the apostles' teaching and to the fellowship, to the breaking of bread and to prayer' but also distinguished themselves when 'selling their possessions and goods, they gave to anyone as he had need' (Acts 2:42,45).

Jackie Pullinger-To, who like Mother Teresa is known for her compassionate work amongst the poor, was once speaking at a conference: 'I hear people crying out, "More Lord. Give me more Lord. I need more, Lord" but I know what their problem is.' She paused and we all held our breath. 'They're always going to be hungry for more because they are all on the wrong diet.'

Jackie's point was clear. Genuine Christian faith is robust and satisfying. Only imitations leave us dissatisfied and perpetually hungry for 'more'. Jesus calls us very simply to: 'Love the Lord your God with all your heart and with all your soul and with all your strength and with all your mind' and to 'Love your neighbour as yourself.' Do this, he says, 'and you will live' (Lk. 10:27-28). Authentic biblical spirituality – the sort that satisfies our souls and fulfils our lives – invariably combines the dual heartbeat of passion for the Lord and compassion for the lost, intimacy with God and involvement in society.

Christians have tended to divide themselves into two groups by temperament. Some of us are naturally contemplative and want to emphasise 'intimacy with God' and others are more activist and are focused on 'involvement in community'; some champion prayer and listening to God and others campaign for engagement and action; some preach 'Wait on the Lord' and others retort 'But let's get on with it!'

Activists often caricature those that are 'so spiritually minded they are no earthly good', but Jesus himself clearly reprimanded Martha for busying herself in the kitchen, lost in a flurry of activity, while affirming her apparently lazy sister, saying: 'only one thing is needed. Mary has chosen what is better, and it will not be taken away from her' (Lk. 10:42). It's easy to imagine Jesus addressing many contemporary Marthas, people who do more *for* Jesus than they do *with* him, in just the same way. 'You are worried and upset about many things,' he might whisper kindly, noting our passion for social justice, cultural relevance or whatever, 'but only one thing is needed.' Mary, like mystics and contemplatives down the ages, clearly had a propensity towards getting 'lost in wonder, love and praise.' On another occasion, while Martha was once again serving dinner, Mary poured about a pint of perfume on Jesus' feet and Judas, for various dubious reasons, was outraged by such extravagance. But Jesus says 'Leave her alone... You will always have the poor among you, but you will not always have me' (Jn.12:7,8).

Those, like Mary, who love to worship with extravagant and apparently irrelevant acts of devotion, remind us that we are no longer to be known as Christ's servants – instead he has named us his friends. Of course it's easy to hide from prayer because it can be so difficult! Don Carson, in his book *A Call to Spiritual Reformation* writes:

> I doubt if there is any Christian who has not sometimes found it difficult to pray. In itself this is neither surprising nor depressing: it is not surprising because we are still pilgrims with many lessons to learn; it is not depressing, because struggling with such matters is part of the way we learn. What is both surprising and depressing is the sheer prayerless-ness that characterises so much of the Western church. It is surprising, because it is out of step with the Bible that portrays what Christian living should be; it is depressing because it frequently co-exists with abounding Christian activity that somehow seems hollow, frivolous and superficial. Scarcely less disturbing is the enthusiastic

praying in some circles that overflows with emotional release but is utterly uncontrolled by any thoughtful reflection on the prayers of Scripture … I wish I could say I always avoid these pitfalls. The truth is that I am part of what I condemn … [2]

Lesslie Newbigin, the great theologian and missionary, observes that 'the great project of bringing heaven down to earth always results in bringing hell up from below.' Our call as agents of the kingdom of heaven on earth is first and foremost to love God exclusively and intimately. People like Jackie Pullinger-To and Mother Teresa remind us that such priorities need not divorce us from reality, nor maroon the church in oceans of social irrelevance. Quite the reverse. From intimacy we are propelled into involvement. This is the heart of God who 'so loved' our world that 'he gave'. It is illustrated in the abandoned sexual intimacy that gives birth to new life – and every parent knows how very practical that can be!

Of course, on the flip-side, while activists all too easily dismiss worshippers as socially irrelevant, it's perhaps even easier for the Marys of this world to entrench themselves on the moral high ground, dismissing the Marthas as legalists, unbelieving workaholics and spiritually superficial. And so, as we caricature one another, the Body of Christ is torn between intimacy and involvement when both dimensions of discipleship are essential to healthy Christianity and fruitful communities. It's like the left hand blaming the right for being on a different side of the body.

This dichotomy has nothing to do with the Bible. Whilst the New Testament urges us to keep our eyes fixed on Jesus, it never does so at the expense of real engagement in the 'here and now'. Intimacy with God and involvement with society are inseparably connected. Prayer and engagement go together – they fuel and sustain one another.

The legal expert who quizzed Jesus about eternal life in Luke 10 seems to have been happy about the call to love God with complete abandonment, yet defensive about the implications of loving his neighbour. Wanting to justify himself he asks Jesus about the definition of the term 'neighbour' and Jesus responds by telling the outrageous story of the Good Samaritan who shames upstanding Jews with acts of lavish mercy towards a traveller who's been mugged on the Jerusalem to Jericho road.

Once again, in this parable, we see the expression of passion for God in practical compassion towards the urgent needs of our neighbour. The apostle John put it like this: 'Anyone who claims to be in the light but hates his brother is still in the darkness. Whoever loves his brother lives in the light, and there is nothing in him to make him stumble. But whoever hates his brother is in the darkness and walks around in the darkness' (1 Jn. 2:9-11). It's not that we are 'getting one bit right' when we 'love' God whilst ignoring the needs of the community, but rather that we are walking around 'in the darkness' whilst claiming to know God. In failing to love our neighbour, we reveal that we do not really love God either.

True intimacy with God and depth in prayer are both the outcome of and the inspiration for our involvement in his world. We pray in order to change the world, but we change the world in order that people might one day bow the knee in prayer (Phil. 2:10). Prophetic involvement in God's world invariably flows from genuine intimacy with and reliance upon God. Intimacy and involvement must belong together – to ignore one is always to destroy the quality and power of the other. An effective church will always be one that is committed to intimacy as well as involvement, because biblical spirituality is integrated spirituality. Outward engagement is as essential as inner orientation. Both are essential if the church is to fulfil its role – representing God to creation.

Faithworks and 24-7 Prayer have teamed up to bring you this resource because both movements are wholly committed to the intimacy and involvement principle. This book is designed to be a 'how-to' guide, used by local churches who share the same vision – that of developing a depth in prayer which both leads to, and flows from, a depth of community engagement. It is filled with ideas to resource you through an entire week of non-stop, night-and-day creative prayer or, if you are not quite ready for that, any prayer event which is appropriate to you. The contents are ideally suited for use during the week leading up to Pentecost but are equally appropriate for any time of the year. You can stick to using the programme exactly as we have set it out or pick-and-mix to produce your own tailor-made version. The key is flexibility – it's really up to you to use as much or as little of the content as you choose. One important principle is that the Prayerworks week of prayer is designed to conclude with an act of commitment on the last Sunday, to a renewed engagement with your community through signing the Faithworks Charter.

When Jesus strode through Galilee and challenged people to 'Repent!' his meaning was clear. He meant 'live your life like me, align yourself with my agenda, heal the sick, liberate the oppressed – love God and love your neighbour.' For these are the signs of the kingdom of God, the incontrovertible evidence of his presence. Following Christ was never about merely tipping your cap to a set of sound, but lifeless, doctrines only to carry on regardless. It was, and remains, a call to a life of both worship and witness, prayerful withdrawal and practical engagement, *intimacy and involvement*, that the world might see that the kingdom of God is here; that the simplest prayer works because Christ reigns on high.

Steve Chalke MBE   **Pete Greig**
Founder Oasis Global and Faithworks   Founder 24-7 Prayer

[1] Published by Ballantine Books, 1995

[2] Don Carson, *A Call to Spiritual Reformation,* (Leicester IVP, 1992)

PART 1:

HOW TO RUN A 24-7 PRAYER ROOM

1 INTRODUCTION
- START HERE!

On the desk in front of me is *Time* magazine's profoundly distressing special report on the tsunami that flooded countless coastlines across Asia and Africa, and stunned the world, on Boxing Day 2004. As the death toll and the donation figures have risen sharply, so have the number of newspaper articles asking questions about 'faith': 'Where is God when people suffer like this?' When interviewed, the Archbishop of Canterbury, Rowan Williams, acknowledged that this question was being asked and then added, 'Indeed, it would be wrong if it weren't.'

And yet, perhaps to the surprise of the journalist, he then appealed for continued faith in God. 'That is also why the reaction of faith is or should be always one of *passionate engagement* with the lives that are left,' he offered, 'a response that asks not for understanding but for ways of changing the situation in whatever perhaps very small ways that are open to us.' This is good news – to engage with passion, to *do something* as a response of *love*. For God so loved the world that he gave … and so should I, because every person on this planet is my neighbour.

The purpose of this book is very simple. It is to encourage people, as individuals, groups and communities, to *passionately engage* with God in prayer – to risk the joy and the pain of intimacy with our Father and Creator God. And then to *passionately engage* with God's world – to express the justice and the mercy and the passion of Jesus into all of creation.

A few years ago, I was asked to lead a joint churches Easter service in our local park. As the PA gear was assembled and people from around the town gathered, so did the clouds. For some strange reason, as the first few specks of rain fell from the sky, I felt a surge of faith and invited everyone to join me in praying for the rain to go and for the sun to shine. As I confidently prayed those words into the microphone, the heavens opened and it absolutely bucketed down. People scattered in every direction as the desperate PA team tried to salvage their soggy gear. I just stood there, feeling quite foolish.

I'm no expert at prayer, which is perhaps why I find 24-7 Prayer rooms helpful. I love the freedom and the space to express what I want to, in the way that I want to, knowing that God is valuing every second as much as I am. I remember visiting my first 24-7 Prayer room, late in 1999, and being immediately overwhelmed by the incredible artwork, the inspiring poetry and painted prayers, the energy and sense of momentum generated by the others praying elsewhere in the room. And I remember wondering, on more than one occasion, if this was anything like what the disciples experienced in their 'upper room', somewhere in Jerusalem, almost two thousand years ago.

A short while after Jesus had been 'taken up before their very eyes' (Acts 1:9) into the sky, the disciples returned to Jerusalem where they joined 'together constantly in prayer, along with the women and Mary the mother of Jesus, and with his brothers' (Acts 1:14). Everyone was together. Scripture *doesn't* say how they all felt and nor does it say what they were praying about. I suspect that the wonder and thrill of their hilltop experience had faded or given way, at least a little, to questions about the future, to confusion and maybe even to some fear. All we do know for sure is that this group of family and friends waited and prayed and waited and prayed, together, not really knowing what they were waiting and praying for, except that it was for the One Jesus had promised, his Holy Spirit.

On Pentecost day, 'Suddenly a sound like the blowing of a violent wind came from heaven and filled the whole house where they were sitting ... All of them were filled with the Holy Spirit' (Acts 2:2,4). As a direct result, they were catapulted out into the marketplace, where they all began speaking in different languages, telling anyone who would listen about the wonders of Jesus. In the minutes that followed, many of the hearers chose to accept that what they were seeing and hearing was true, and they began to cry out, 'What shall we do?' (Acts 2:37). Typically, it was Peter who spoke up with the answer! Incredible miracles began to take place – the sick were healed and the demonised were set free, just as Jesus had promised – and the initial group of believers grew rapidly. Scripture says that these believers 'devoted themselves to the apostles' teaching and to the fellowship, to the breaking of bread and to prayer' (Acts 2:42). As they prayed, signs and wonders continued to follow and acts of justice and mercy began to take place as well. Money was distributed more fairly; 'selling their possessions and goods, they gave to anyone as he had need' (Acts 2:45, 4:35), and the vulnerable were cared for more kindly (Acts 6:1-4).

These are *all* signs of the kingdom of God – salvation, healings and miracles, acts of justice and mercy. This is the subject that Jesus spoke of, told stories about, and demonstrated more than any other. When Jesus stood up in the synagogue, to the horror of the people, and read from the Isaiah 61 scroll, he described the coming of the kingdom of God – good news to the poor, freedom for the prisoners, sight for the blind, release for the oppressed, and proclamation of the year of the Lord's favour (Lk. 4:18-19). Forget Christmas cards for a moment, *this* is what true 'peace on earth' – *shalom* – is all about, and all of creation is groaning and yearning for us to embrace this purpose, this 'calling' and to participate with God in it (Rom. 8:19).

Jesus was very clear about his purpose, his 'calling'. He came for the poor and the sick, for those who needed him – he healed them, fed them, listened to them and touched them, forgave them and restored them. 'It is not the healthy who need a doctor,' he said, 'but the sick' (Mt. 9:12), and Jesus beckons us onto this path with a purpose. 'Come, follow me' he asks firmly, and so we do.

Jesus surprised the religious leaders again by summarising the Ten Commandments into just two: 'Love the Lord your God with all your heart and with all your soul and with all your mind' and 'Love your neighbour as yourself.' He then added a story, just in case anyone was unclear who their 'neighbour' might be. The 'Good Samaritan' parable (Lk.10:25-37) is still a profoundly exciting and challenging story (no matter how many versions you've read, heard or seen performed!), because it not only tells us *who* our neighbours are (anyone in need), but also *how to act* towards them; with kindness, generosity and selflessness. Love must act. In *Red Moon Rising*, Pete Greig describes religion without action as 'religion in hiding'. He acknowledges that Jesus' own mission statement was to 'preach good news to the poor, and he didn't just long for it, he left Heaven and did it!'

I know it's really tempting to just skip past Scripture quotes, especially if they're familiar ones, and if they're a bit long like this next one is, but please resist the temptation to do so. If possible, try to read these few verses through a couple of times, and then maybe put the book down for a few minutes to let the words sink in.

Is this not the kind of fasting I have chosen: to loose the chains of injustice and untie the cords of the yoke, to set the oppressed free and break every yoke? Is it not to share your food with the hungry and to provide the poor wanderer with shelter – when you see the naked, to clothe him, and not to turn away from your own flesh and blood? Then your light will break forth like the dawn, and your healing will quickly appear; then your righteousness will go before you, and the glory of the Lord will be your rearguard. Then you will call, and the Lord will answer; you will cry for help, and he will say: Here am I. If you do away with the yoke of oppression, with the pointing finger and malicious talk, and if you spend yourselves on behalf of the hungry and satisfy the needs of the oppressed, then your light will rise in the darkness ...'

(Isaiah 58:6-10)

THE BIGGEST MIRACLE

The great Baptist preacher C.H. Spurgeon, writing in a book entitled *Effective Prayer*, observed that 'Prayer itself is an art which only the Holy Ghost can teach us. He is the giver of all prayer. Pray for prayer – pray till you can pray; pray to be helped to pray, and give not up praying because you cannot pray, for it is when you think you cannot pray that you are most praying.'

Over the last five years, many of those who have spent time in 24-7 Prayer rooms around the world have been doing little more than *learning* to pray (myself included). Nevertheless, we've prayed like never before – with laughter and tears and 'groans that words cannot express' (Rom. 8:26), in churches and youth centres, schools and colleges, derelict warehouses and disused pubs. Countless stories have emerged from these contemporary upper rooms – stories of profound encounters with God, of salvation and healing, of renewal, reconciliation and acts of kindness.

Perhaps the biggest miracle, though, has been the changes in *us*, those who have prayed. We've found ourselves propelled from prayer rooms into our homes and schools and streets with a deeper desire to *be good news* in all kinds of creative ways. We've also found ourselves launched out onto mission teams around the world, to the drug-fuelled clubs and bars of Ibiza, for example, where we've talked and prayed with clubbers while giving out free fruit and clearing dirty beaches. And we've found ourselves establishing Boiler Rooms, modern-day monasteries with a particular focus on prayer, mission and justice (more on this later).

> *Clearing up Sarah's vomit a few minutes later, Penny reflected that this was not quite what any of them had anticipated when they first imagined a 24-7 house of prayer … (But) maybe this is what prayer is all about. One minute you're kneeling in quiet contemplation, the next you're kneeling by an unconscious girl; one day you talk to God about people and the next you talk to people about God. This marriage of intimacy with active involvement in a hurting world is the very meaning of the word intercession.*
>
> Taken from *Red Moon Rising*, by Pete Greig and Dave Roberts [3]

THE CLOUD OF WITNESSES

In Hebrews chapter 11, the writer tells stories of Old Testament heroes of the faith who are part of the 'great cloud of witnesses' in heaven (Heb. 12:1). We might be comforted by the fact that most of these 'heroes' were spectacular failures (comforted, because we consider ourselves to be such failures too!), but we will definitely be deeply challenged by their faith in action in the moments when it really mattered. As the years have passed, this crowd has swelled considerably. Imagine, if you will, the scene …

> A group have gathered around Jeremiah and Isaiah, encouraging them to repeat some of their prophecies, and they rise to the occasion. Jeremiah declares, 'to defend the cause of the poor and the needy … that is what it means to know the Lord!' With barely a pause, Isaiah immediately adds, 'Seek justice, encourage the oppressed. Defend the cause of the fatherless, plead the cause of the widow … Stop bringing meaningless offerings!' Tertullian nods in agreement, suggesting that, just as in the early church, these offerings should be used 'to support and bury poor people, to supply the wants of needy boys and girls without parents, and of housebound old people'. Next to him, Iraneus remembers that, 'instead of tithes which the law commanded, the Lord said to divide everything we have with the poor … giving joyfully and freely, and not just the least valuable of … possessions'. James summarises the thoughts of his friends with a line from his letter, 'Religion that God our Father accepts as pure and faultless is this: to look after orphans and widows in their distress and to keep oneself from being polluted by the world' (See Is.1:17,13a, Tertullian's *Apology 39*, Iraneus's *Against Heresies 4.13.3*, Jas. 1:27).

Just along from James, however, Micah is also reminding us what the Lord requires, 'to act justly and to love mercy and to walk humbly with your God' (Mich. 6:8). The group around him are clearly eager to tell their stories and encourage us to be passionate in our prayer and action too. Firstly, Catherine and William Booth tell of times in meetings when 'people were struck down, overwhelmed with a sense of the presence and power of God', before urging us to care for the poor as their Salvation Army does. Then Wilberforce talks about his friends in Clapham, and how their prayer and encouragement helped him to remain true to what God had called him to – to see slavery abolished in England. And finally Wesley begins to tell of his encounter with Zinzendorf and the Moravians, and his subsequent ministry to the poor in London. But he is interrupted by the eccentric Count himself, and Wesley suggests that Zinzendorf 'tell the one hundred-year prayer meeting story.' We feel a fire kindling inside us as we listen to the extraordinary stories of seemingly endless night and day prayer, which launched missionaries across the world, even some who sold themselves into slavery simply to reach slaves with the good news of Jesus. Some of those missionaries and pray-ers add their words to the story as it unfolds, until a hush settles across the great 'cloud' of witnesses. And Jesus begins to speak some familiar words … 'Blessed are the poor in spirit …'

He finishes, a few minutes later, with an excited shout as he points at us, 'You are the light of the world … let your light shine before men, that they may see your good deeds and praise your Father in heaven' (Mt. 5:14-16). He then points beyond us, to the world, to the millions of 'sheep without a shepherd', and he says, 'Ask the Lord of the harvest … to send out workers into his harvest field' (Mt.9: 36-38). Pray! A roar erupts from the crowd, as these great heroes of the faith, along with countless angels, begin to clap and cheer us onward, bewildered and humbled as we are … to run the race!

AND SO LET US PRAY

The history of significant moves of God on the earth (from the Welsh revival to the Azusa Street event) reveals something with inescapable clarity – the tide turns through moments and movements of continual prayer.

God hears and responds to the sacrificial, day-and-night prayers of ordinary people like you and I. Like a wave drawing back from the shore, gathering in energy for its moment to crest, turn and crash upon the shore, people across the earth are also gathering their prayers. In churches from every stream and denomination, in schools and workplaces, in homes and on the streets, in prisons and in Parliament, people are praying like never before. A moment will soon come when this wave crests and turns – and for that we cry, 'Come on!'

As we read the Pentecost story, the day when God's people around the world remember the extraordinary outpouring of Holy Spirit 'on all flesh', and the birth of the Church, we find that this 'all flesh' is flesh just like ours. The week of night-and-day, 24 hour prayer for which this book has been designed echoes that story. It encourages us to make time for seeking God, for asking God some honest questions and listening carefully for God's direction; time to defy the acceleration of our busy lives and wait on God, time for intimacy with the Father and time to be energised once again by the Holy Spirit, to respond to God's call to be involved, to be *passionately engaged* in our communities and our world.

And just in case you're wondering, this is not just for the expert pray-ers, this is for 'all flesh', for people just like you and I. So, welcome on board – enjoy the journey!

> *Above the door-frame that led out of the 24-7 Prayer room, someone had stuck a large sign with the word, 'WELCOME' painted across it. As we left the room, at whatever time of day or night, we were reminded that God was not only eager to meet with us in the prayer room, but that God was also beckoning us out into the routines of the day, into the pleasures and the struggles – that God wanted to meet with us there too.*

ANON

---

[3] Pete Greig and Dave Roberts, *Red Moon Rising*, (Eastbourne, Kingsway, 2004)

2 WHAT IS 24-7 PRAYER?
– A (VERY) BRIEF STORY-SO-FAR

'Be joyful always; pray continually.' (1 Thes. 5:16-17)

Right now, as you're reading this sentence, someone, somewhere is praying in a 24-7 Prayer room. In fact, many people are. As I write this sentence the www.24-7prayer.com web-diary shows that *fourteen* 24-7 Prayer rooms across six nations are praying … right now. And experience suggests that there are probably many more who haven't registered. Since September 1999 an unbroken chain of prayer rooms have prayed night and day. With thanksgiving and desperation, praise and anguish, people all over the world have been seeking God and wrestling in prayer in little prayer rooms much like the one that you're about to set up.

24-7 Prayer is both a model and a movement. It is a model in the sense that it offers a flexible way for groups and for churches to pray. Part 1 of this book (and the various other resources listed at the back of the book) will provide a good how-to guide to getting your prayer room started.

24-7 Prayer is also a movement, in the sense that as you get started you will be joining in with many thousands of others, from over 56 different nations, who are on this same journey. As you pray, you will be sharing space with other ordinary people, praying in all kinds of weird and wonderful places.

Like many movements, 24-7 Prayer started almost by accident. But it started nonetheless and it hasn't stopped since, in spite of the number of times we've wondered if it might. Dare I say this? It feels and seems like something that God is inspiring.

A BRIEF HISTORY OF 24-7 PRAYER

- On **5th September 1999**, Revelation Church in Chichester opened their first prayer room. Pete, Samie and one-year-old Hudson Greig had been travelling around Europe during the summer of 1999, and they'd visited Herrnhut in Germany. Pete and Samie came back from their travels inspired and excited by the extraordinary story of the Moravians' one hundred year prayer meeting, wondering if God might be saying something to them. Only a few short weeks later, the first prayer room opened.

In October 1999 I visited Revelation Church one Sunday evening. I felt a bit out of place until a girl came up to us and explained that they'd been doing this thing called 24-7 Prayer for the last two months and did I want to see it? She seemed very excited about showing us. However, all that hit me as we went in was this really bad smell – a kind of 'wet paint 'smell.

I ventured further into the room – there was paper everywhere and it was really messy with things falling off the walls – it was just a bit weird. As I looked around I saw two people lying down with their eyes shut as if they were asleep, and I just thought, what are you doing? It was just strange – I wondered why would anyone want to spend any time in here? Some people who aren't Christians walk into 24-7 Prayer rooms and are hit by the presence of God. I think I was hit by this slightly weird, messy and really smelly bedroom!

PHIL (whose name was on the Chichester prayer room wall as 'someone needing to find God' ... and now works for 24-7 Prayer in the UK, supporting prayer rooms! Miracles do happen!)

- A poem, *The Vision*, appeared on the prayer room wall. A few weeks later it bounced across the world via email, circulated around China's underground church, was published in the United States and choreographed in Spain.

The vision?
The vision is Jesus – obsessively, dangerously,
undeniably Jesus.
The vision is an army of young people.
You see bones? I see an army.

PETE (Chichester)

(This poem, along with some stunning imagery can be found in Pete Greig's book, *Vision and Vow*, Eastbourne: Kingsway, 2005).

- In November 1999, other groups and churches were inspired by stories from the Chichester prayer room at the Cultural Shift gathering in Southampton. Within weeks, many were hosting 24-7 Prayer weeks themselves.

- The www.24-7prayer.com website was also born at this time, enabling groups and churches to register their 24-7 Prayer weeks, to receive encouragement from articles posted on it and to share their stories on the boards.

- From May 2001-May 2002, the Salvation Army in the UK organised its corps to pray 24-7-365, an entire year of unbroken prayer. Many other networks and denominations also followed this model.

Over two hundred centres took part, and the effects on our movement were astounding. As people all over the country used the same model for prayer, we began to see a common heart, a common passion and a common vision for prayer emerging, all the way from the north of Scotland to the Channel Islands. We have never seen anything like it before and God has used it to catapult us into a new phase of prayer-centred mission, which will transform the future of our movement.

LYNDALL (prayer co-ordinator, Salvation Army UK)

- In 2001, the first 24-7 Missions Teams were sent out, in response to invitations to 'take 24-7 Prayer' to such places as Ibiza, Mexico and Germany. Since then, teams have headed all over the world – to Brazil and Belgrade, Ayia Napa and Amsterdam, to rock festivals in Sweden and to the Olympics in Athens, taking prayer and mission and practical serving onto the streets. Read the stories at www.24-7mission.com.

Each night members of the team will go in pairs around the streets of the town, chatting, caring and offering to pray. It's not like a cold calling thing, there are no tracts or pressure. They just see where the conversation goes and offer to pray when they can. The effects are incredible. Just in the weekend I was there

I one woman asked for prayer for her to be able to have a child.

II a young guy, who had come to Napa partly to get away from the faith of his Christian foster parents, met the team, chatted and asked to meet them again.

III a jewellery trader asked for prayer and expressed how it had touched her. She wanted to meet the team again.

IV a man who had had some bad experiences with Christians was able to be prayed for and was amazed at being accepted by the team.

ANDY (Ayia Napa, 2004)

- That same year, the first 24-7 Boiler Room (which sometimes get described as 'Third Millennium Monasteries') launched. Boiler Rooms are prayer-houses at the heart of local communities, hostels for modern-day pilgrims, outlets for justice for the poor, mission stations and arts centres all rolled into one. For more information check www.boiler-rooms.com. Groups and churches are currently dreaming and scheming about Boiler Rooms all over the UK, as well as in Canada, Sweden, South Africa and many other nations.

A young girl who's been coming in regularly to the Reading Boiler Room is quickly discovering a relationship with Jesus. She now prays regularly with a team member and is talking seriously about getting baptised.

Also, we've been asked by the guys that drop in to have a 'God-meeting' plus some (cell) small-groups. Isn't that incredible? Not-yet-Christians asking for a meeting!
ANDY (Reading Boiler Room)

- On 31st December 2002 the Swedish Free Churches completed a year of unbroken 24-7 Prayer. With a Swedish website and Swedish resources designed by a Swedish team, many churches had no idea that the vision had originally come from beyond their shores, which was exciting. Too often 'culture' is exported along with 'vision', and thus indigenous creativity is stifled. From the start we have looked to establish teams and bases that can oversee and develop the movement nationally. To date, 24-7 Prayer rooms have appeared in almost sixty nations worldwide, across five continents. Incredible.

We just finished doing two weeks up here in GP. Our first week we all centred pretty much on ourselves, on what God was doing in us and how we long for him. But our second week had a focus on our city. We placed a newspaper ad and invited people to send in prayer requests, or sign up for slots. We posted the requests in the prayer chapel. I called the mayor and got a prayer request from him. And we had a wall of names, we took post-it notes and had people write names of those they were praying for on the notes, and stick 'em to the wall!

KIM (Sweden)

- In the summer of 2003, the documentary *God Bless Ibiza* was shown on national TV in the UK. Channel 4 later chose it as the documentary they were most proud of at an annual reception for production companies. Since then articles about 24-7 Prayer have appeared in *The Spectator* and *The Times*, and an American prayer room has adorned the front cover of *USA Today*. *Rolling Stone* were going to run a six page article they'd commissioned on 24-7 Prayer, but concluded, at the very last minute, that Christianity was 'not cool enough.'

- During 2004, the pace quickened and the profile rose again, with an unprecedented 24-7 Prayer week in the Houses of Parliament in London. Staff and a few Members of Parliament joined with others around the UK, praying for their colleagues and for the nations. Psalm 127:1 says 'Unless the Lord builds the house, its builders labour in vain.' On Tuesday 8th June, at the very start of the week, we stood on the mosaic in Central Lobby, which is the meeting point of the two Houses, and prayed over this Latin inscription. Its location, and its inclusion in the architecture of the buildings is significant.

- …and so to the present day. This movement shows no signs of slowing!

GOING WITH THE FLOW?

I wonder sometimes if we get so absorbed in our planning and strategising, our scheming and searching for God's 'next big thing', that we miss the obvious (and often extraordinary) ways that God is working in the world around us, in the things that are right in front of our faces.

In the film *Finding Nemo*, two of the main characters, Marlin and Dory, fight their way through a field of jellyfish, only to be stung into unconsciousness. Marlin wakes up on the back of his rescuer, a turtle called Crush, and he immediately begins to panic, aware that their journey has been diverted and their time wasted. 'I must find the EAC!' he blurts out. 'The East Australia Current ... I must find it! Do you know where it is?!' The turtle grins at Marlin over his shoulder and says simply, 'You're riding it, dude!'

There is a global current of prayer, a tide, a rising wave and maybe God is simply inviting us to 'ride it ... (dudes?!)'

The next part of this journey is yours. The sections that follow will help you to prepare for and practically plan your 24-7 Prayer room.

3 PREPARATION
- GETTING YOUR GROUP OR CHURCH READY

I just noticed these words on the sign next to our prayer room door:
[In Case Of Fire]

In case of fire, know what to do. What should we do in case of God's fire? Get ready, get in place, leave behind all that prevents you from being touched by God's fire. Get ready. Be prepared. PM

Deciding to embark on a 24-7 Prayer week (or fortnight, or month, or even just a day for that matter) is not the same as actually doing it. Preparation and planning are what bridge the gap between deciding and doing, or as someone else has said, between aspiration and achievement.

Groups and churches who have hosted similar weeks of prayer (or other projects) before might find it easier to motivate and organise themselves in preparation for a 24-7 Prayer week. Generally, though, we've found that it takes about two months to do all this from scratch.

GETTING IT

The best way really to understand what a 24-7 Prayer room is like and to catch the vision is to visit one. On the www.24-7prayer.com website, there is a list of who's praying at any time, along with contact details. Maybe you could take a small group from your group or church over to a local prayer room for an evening?

Alternatively, you could make contact with a few of the recent prayer rooms and hear directly from the people who are doing it. Hearing stories from the places that are praying 24-7 is always exciting and encouraging. It could also provide you with an opportunity to ask some questions and to explore the concerns you may have about hosting a 24-7 Prayer room – chances are, they probably shared those same concerns but found ways to overcome them.

Along with this book, there are a number of other publications and sources of information and stories that you and your core group of prayer room planners could make use of – see the Resources section at the back of the book.

LEADERSHIP

In *The Great Divorce*, C. S. Lewis's storyteller describes being in the heavenly country, a place of dazzling light and colour. As he sits with his guide, they watch a beautiful woman ...

"emerge from a nearby wood, surrounded by a procession of animals and angels, all honouring her with songs and music and petals cast before her feet. The storyteller feels breathless and barely able to move. He wonders who this great woman might be – perhaps a saint? Perhaps Mary, the mother of Jesus herself? His guide however, sensing the potential for mistaken identity, explains that this beautiful woman is someone that the storyteller will have never heard of - he mentions her name and then describes her love and kindness for everyone she met. Perhaps still sensing the storyteller's confusion at such honour offered to someone so 'normal', the guide explains that fame in the heavenly country is quite different to fame on earth."

Names and fame matter very little in the kingdom of God. The night hours in 24-7 Prayer rooms all over the world are scattered with the kingdom's never-heard-of heroes. Nonetheless, the 'name and fame' of your local group or church leaders will prove important in the early stages of *preparing* for a 24-7 Prayer week.

In her report on the Salvation Army's first year of 24-7 Prayer, Lyndall Bywater noted that they 'found it very helpful to ask their national leaders to commend the year of prayer, even before it had begun, as this excited the enthusiasts and reassured the sceptics.' The same is true of a local 24-7 Prayer room. Exciting the enthusiasts and reassuring the sceptics are both important.

So, at an early stage, put this book into the hands of the leaders of your group or church. Encourage them to visit a 24-7 Prayer room or talk to someone who's been involved in one, and introduce them to the other resources that are available. They may not be the best people to *organise* the week of prayer but their commendation and involvement will be important.

GET A TEAM

Then get a team together. As you'll soon discover (if you haven't already guessed), there's quite a lot of preparation to do. You'll need a small team of people who are all really enthusiastic about making your 24-7 Prayer week happen and you'll need to have the following skills amongst this team:

• communication (see next heading)

• creativity (see the chapter on creative prayer, and Part 2 of this book)

• administration/organisation (for keeping the whole process rolling smoothly and particularly for co-ordinating the rota)

Don't worry, there's lots to do for others who don't feel specifically skilled in any of these areas as well. So get your team together, get them praying together, read this book and share ideas together, and go for it!

COMMUNICATION: TALK, TELL, TEASE ...

Of course, you could create the *most* awe-inspiring 24-7 Prayer room but if people are not inspired and motivated to come and pray, then all the effort will be wasted. What takes the most time and creative thought, prior to the launch of a 24-7 Prayer room, is *communication*. How are you going to get your friends, the others in your group or church, on board? How are you going to inspire and mobilise them enough to sign their names onto your 24-7 Prayer rota and turn up at 3am on that Tuesday morning (or whenever) to pray?

You might want to start by getting your small team to think about the various means of communication in your group or church, i.e.

- newsletters
- emails and group-mails
- text messages
- Sunday (or whenever) meeting notices
- small (cell or house) groups
- noticeboards
- other groups – youthgroups, parents and toddlers, children's clubs, etc.
- web-based discussion boards

You might then think about what kind of things you will need to communicate:

- the broad vision of 24-7 Prayer
- what a 24-7 Prayer room might look like (photos could be useful)
- some history – day-and-night prayer in Scripture, through church history, and especially amongst the Moravian church in the 1700s
- the details of your week and how it fits into the national setting – dates, times, when it starts and finishes, ...and where it will take place
- how a 24-7 Prayer week works – signing up on the rota, etc.
- why a 24-7 Prayer room works, i.e. why pray in a room? (See next chapter for more on this important question.)

You might even want to tie this in with a broader teaching and training season centred around prayer and mission (intimacy and involvement), or prayer and fasting, or hearing God and responding to God, or creativity and the prophetic in prayer, or any number of other themes. Teaching around the scriptural interconnectedness of prayer and action/mission would be a healthy place to start for most churches!

In preparation for our 24-7 Prayer week I asked the leadership team for a five minute slot in every Sunday meeting for two months to explain different aspects of the week. For a lot of leadership teams (pastors, vicars, priests, etc.) this could be like asking for the keys to the safe, so be prepared for some negotiation. (It's like selling a house – start the bidding as high as you can, but be willing to settle for less.) Returning to what I said earlier, my experience is that this is where you *must* have leaders on board, championing the prayer week as much as you are.

Each week I also read out a story from a 24-7 Prayer room that had taken place that week, to emphasise that *our* week was part of something far bigger than us. I also produced a very simple handout – a different one each week – with a summary of what I'd explained that Sunday, a story or two, something from Scripture about prayer, and a taster of what next week's slot would be about. Gradually the momentum built, and by the time our 24-7 Prayer week was about to launch, the church were ready – ready to sign up, turn up and get praying!

It's a bit like drip-feeding. You will need to find the best ways to feed people just enough to keep them interested and gradually get them excited, without them feeling overloaded (and overfed) and scared. You might want to try different methods, even during a meeting slot, i.e. different people doing the communicating, inviting someone from a previous 24-7 Prayer room to tell their stories, doing it as an interview, etc.

And let me say this one more time – stories are incredibly valuable. We grow in faith when we hear stories of people, who are just like us, meeting God in ways that we imagine that we could too. So, encourage people in your group or church to use the website regularly, or sign up to the UK Report email – and encourage them to start sharing their stories as well.

At first I didn't think that I could pray for a whole hour. I wondered what I could possibly pray about. But I closed my eyes and I prayed all my feelings to God and the hour went past in a flash!

Once again, I want you, God, to know that I'm sorry for all the bad things I've done. I will try my best to love others the way that you love me. I pray that I will try my hardest to forgive others, just like how you always forgive me. Help me to live like Jesus each day, and I wanna tell you, I LOVE YOU GOD! Amen.

Love, Sharon (13)

Praise God for 24-7. I wasn't sure about being involved in this week, but it's *electric*, I cannot keep away. (The only problem is, I keep talking about it at work – bless them, they try to understand when I say the alarm clocks go at all different times day and night to get to the 24-7 Prayer *room!) God, I acknowledge your existence. I know what I have to do. I need your help Jesus. I have got out of the way of praying – help me this week. I love you – help me pray.*

I am loving being in this room, in the presence of God, somewhere to come after work, during the night, just to be near to my Dad.

ANON

3, 2, 1 ... BLAST OFF!!

The countdown has ended. Weeks of communicating and envisioning have brought you and your group or church to the launch pad, your launch event. It's like an athlete – having completed months of training, which have affected her lifestyle, routines and diet and, well, almost everything – she has now arrived at the starting line, completely *prepared* and ready ... and ... *bang!!*

Make sure that your 24-7 Prayer week starts well. Some churches use an existing meeting or service to 'kick-start' it (as many who are using the pre-Pentecost week will probably do, starting at midday on the previous Sunday). Whatever you do though, make sure that, like the starting gun firing for the one hundred metres final, it focuses everyone's attention and increases their anticipation. Here are a few ideas that you might like to consider:

- Famous people (and some less famous!) occasionally get invited to launch new ships or open new shops – they give a short speech and then smash a bottle of champagne or cut a ribbon. You could invite someone to do something similar – maybe someone involved in a previous 24-7 Prayer week, maybe a well-known local church leader or an 'unknown' child? (If you have developed a good relationship with the Local Authority, you could even invite the local mayor, or a local headteacher or business leader to open your prayer room? If you do, be very clear what you're asking them to do.)

- The Olympics opens with the lighting of the Olympic Flame. Many churches begin their week by lighting a long-burning candle together, as a symbol of the constant prayer that is about to begin in the room, and a picture of the ever-burning fire in the temple (Lev. 6:13).

- Periods of fasting and prayer undertaken by many religions begin (and end) with a celebratory meal. You could invite your whole group or church to gather (either in the prayer room or somewhere nearby) for a celebratory meal together, or to share the 'Lord's Supper' together, or simply to worship and celebrate the goodness of God.

There are probably hundreds of creative ways to launch a week of 24-7 Prayer. The important thing is that you do it *together*. In spite of the fact that at any given hour during the week there may only be one or two people in the prayer room, the week belongs to your *whole* group or church community. They need to try to be there for the launch and the close, as well as in between!

In my first 24-7 Prayer room there were about thirty of us at the launch. We counted down the seconds, like at a shuttle-launch or in anticipation of Big Ben's 12 o'clock chimes at New Year, and at the very moment when our week began, we all prayed together, as loudly as we could. It was fantastic.

I'll say more about this in the next chapter, but it helps to have your 24-7 Prayer week rota pinned up somewhere prominently at the launch (in fact, throughout the week), so that people can sign themselves up for slots at the last minute. Many people are nervous about signing themselves up to pray for an hour … that is until they get into the prayer room for the first time. Once there, they begin to join in those first few minutes of prayer and all of a sudden they realise that the God who is everywhere has been waiting for them right there.

KEEP GOING ...

Having started, a 24-7 Prayer room tends to take on a life of its own. Artwork spreads across the walls (if you're allowing that kind of creative anarchy!), poetry and sculptures appear, the prayer-log fills with prayers of praise (and some of anguish too) … and it can get quite messy!

Almost (in)famously now, Pete Greig admits that he tried to close the very first 24-7 Prayer room in Chichester in 1999 – he felt concerned that the enthusiasm for prayer might soon fizzle out, and therefore suggested that it would probably be better to close with people left wanting more. Needless to say, the prayer room that Pete was a part of continued, and the rest is (recent) history.

You could, however, fuel the prayer room some more by watching out for particularly encouraging stories, Scriptures or prophetic words and making a feature of them. You could copy them and email them to others in your group or church, or deliver them to small group leaders to read in their meetings and thus hopefully encourage more participation. It probably won't take much, but encourage people to talk about what they experience in the prayer room - you will find that their faith is contagious and the 'fire' will spread.

> *I asked you to give me people to talk to about you, and you have! I prayed for people to ask me questions about you Lord and the next day it happened. I don't know how it started but I found myself talking to two guys at college about what I believed!!*
>
> BEN

...BUT DON'T BURN OUT

On 22nd August 2004 I sat in front of my television staring in utter disbelief – Paula Radcliffe, the incredible marathon runner and probably the favourite for a gold medal, had suddenly stopped running! She looked exhausted and terribly upset. After twenty-three of the twenty-six miles, she just couldn't run any further. She slowed down and just collapsed onto the roadside, with her head in her hands. In an interview later that day, one of the other British runners expressed her sympathy, and ended by saying; 'Maybe she just underestimated the course?'

A week of 24-7 Prayer is 168 hours, which is a *lot* of hours. Even with all the preparation and communication and lots of enthusiasm and a team to help organise it, etc., you might still get half way through the week and find that you've 'underestimated the course'. It *might* turn out to be just that little bit too far. If you do, stop. Or, if possible, just slow down. Thankfully, 24-7 Prayer is not a race.

I certainly don't want to discourage you from aiming for a full 168-hour 24-7 Prayer week, because there's lots to gain from stretching beyond our own resources and into God's, but do please consider these reflections from Lyndall Bywater:

> We quickly learnt not to be too 'precious' about the 24-7 concept. Prayer is the key thing, and as much of it as possible, but otherwise, God honours creativity and determination and so should we. Once we had dropped our legalistic attachment to certain aspects of the 24-7 concept, we were hugely blessed to watch the hundreds of new ways in which people got round the obstacles. Where possible, we very strongly urged people to stick to the 'normal' idea (168 hours of non-stop prayer in one room), but those who had to deviate from that idea for any reason were not disappointed.

(Chapter 6 of this section will explore a few alternatives for groups/churches who genuinely feel that a 24-7 Prayer week is presently beyond their capacity.)

...SPLASH DOWN!

Starting and finishing well are both important, although you *will* need to leave the race analogy behind if you are to end your 24-7 Prayer week in a healthy way. It is very tempting to want to 'win', to summarise the successes, to draw life-changing conclusions, to reduce the journey down to 'What worked' and 'What didn't'or to ask 'In what way was our 24-7 Prayer week a success?' Try to resist this temptation. There will be ample time for a more objective review and evaluation of the week a little later, an honest look at the successes *and* the failures, but firstly you need to gather stories and celebrate.

At the end of every 24-7 Prayer week that I have been involved in, we have invited the whole church community to come and squeeze into our little prayer room for the final two hours. We take it in turns to share what we have learnt and heard from God, what has inspired us and excited us, where God has answered prayers and where we are still wrestling with unanswered prayers, what we've been deeply moved by and what we've found hilariously funny (there are always some funny stories!), who we've been encouraged by and what we feel God changing in our individual lives. This has been our closing ceremony. Just like at the Olympics, where the winners and losers all join the final parade and share in the collective moment of celebration, we all offer what we have experienced. Then, like fireworks being released to mark and celebrate the very end, we all pray together and we send our gratitude into the heavens.

> At the end of our 24-7 Prayer week, we crammed ourselves into the prayer room – there were about fifty people from different churches there – and we began to share our stories as usual. My two daughters, Megan (5) and Poppy (3), were there too, having enjoyed participating in the prayer room throughout the week. About half way through the storytelling, my wife got their pyjamas on and was trying to remove them from the room and get them home for bed. Poppy, being the 'performer', was reluctant to leave … and to the amusement of many, she started to go up to people, one after another, and kiss them lightly on the lips. It was distracting. But it was also quite funny. I tried to share one of my stories, but Poppy's kissing-tour was gradually attracting more attention and causing more amusement. I watched her, kissing people she knew, and people she didn't, smiling all the time … and then others began to watch too. Suddenly it seemed like God was there. Through Poppy's innocent kisses, suddenly we were aware of God's kisses; God's grateful kisses. God's wordless love, expressed in the kiss of a child.
>
> PHIL

You could equally end your week with a meal together, or a bonfire (with fireworks?), or a time of worship and singing, or a party, or any number of ways that more significantly reflect your departure from the prayer room.

INTIMACY AND INVOLVEMENT

For those who have planned their 24-7 Prayer week to finish on Pentecost Sunday, you have a story pregnant with imagery and creativity to draw from and pray into. You will need to find a way to express your 'bursting out' of the prayer room and into the streets of your local community. Hopefully, some of the resources and ideas in the third section of this book will inspire you to do just that – prayer *and* action, intimacy *and* involvement.

4 PLANNING
- GETTING YOUR PRAYER ROOM READY

I knew that the compulsion would come. As my head fell back onto my pillow, I knew that my spiritual tiredness was greater than my physical tiredness. I knew that I would find no rest in my bed. I knew that I had to be in this room. The room where a fire is burning, where a stove is waiting. I knew there would be copious food and drink to satisfy the most hungry and thirsty. So I came. To find rest. And I began to feel the peace ooze through my body, melting the pain ... crushing, searing pain ... heartache ... tiredness ... hurt.

ANON

WHY PRAY IN A ROOM?

'Why can't I pray in my own home? It's safer, it's warmer, and it's more convenient.'

If you intend to go ahead and set up a 24-7 Prayer room for your group or church, then you will, at some point, be asked this question or one very similar to it, and you'll hear some of these objections.

The answer to the question is (of course), 'You can if you want to! You can pray *anywhere*! Yes, your home is probably safer, it is probably warmer, and almost definitely, it is more convenient.' We want to encourage everyone to pray more, wherever they are. Paul encourages us to 'pray continually' (1 Thes. 5:16-17) – that means at home, at work, in college, on holiday, when we're travelling and when we're standing still ... it definitely doesn't *just* mean when we're in a prayer room.

The early Celtic Christians were great at this – they even developed prayers for the most mundane aspects of their daily lives, such as making their beds and digging the gardens. But this was because they had a theology which truly embraced the God who was in all, over all and through all. They knew Jesus Christ 'who fills everything in every way' (Eph. 1:23). They believed that the earth was indeed *full* of God's glory, and that God was indeed whispering in different ways through it all. Prayer and action went hand in hand for them; we have a lot still to learn from these disciples.

Someone has said that 'God speaks to the hearer far more than through the speaker'. If we listened more, we would hear God more, in all kinds of surprising ways and places. C. S. Lewis knew this. In *The Problem of Pain* he describes the secret signature of each soul, the thread of beauty in every day of our lives that speaks to our souls, which he identifies as the voice of the Creator, the whisper of heaven.

In his wonderful book, *Life After God*,[4] Douglas Coupland echoes this same idea – he suggests that we all experience daily 'resonant moments', momentary glimpses of breathtaking beauty and uplifting inspiration that make our souls 'vibrate'. And they do. This is the whisper of our Creator God, the God who is in all, and over all, and through all.

Having said all of this, this same Creator God, the God who is everywhere, is sometimes *somewhere*. Ordinary people like you and I have experienced these *somewhere* moments with God in 24-7 Prayer rooms the world over – this is Immanuel, God with us. Although there is no formula to it, when we take a closer look at the pages of this ever more exciting story of 24-7 Prayer rooms from Tulsa, Oklahoma to Tumbi-Umbi, New South Wales, we find patterns beginning to emerge – possible reasons why night and day prayer rooms *work*.

> *There's no room for me in here, it's all you, you, YOU – FANTASTIC! Can it be like this all the time? It's like my heart is coming out of a deep sleep. I feel stirring, groans building, passion, compassion growing!*
> EMMA

#1: Continuity

In a 24-7 Prayer room, people generally sign up for one hour slots. Some may choose to stay and pray for longer (you'll find that many will come back for longer slots later in the week, having experienced their first hour, and then deciding that it was *not enough!*), but most will stick with the one hour slots. (The simple rota system is explained later in this chapter.)

But if everyone prayed independently, in their own homes, using this hourly rota model, there would be almost no sense of *continuity*. You wouldn't know whether the person scheduled to pray before you had actually done so, what they had prayed about, nor, importantly, what they felt God saying to them. You would be starting from scratch every hour.

In a 24-7 Prayer room, continuity, momentum and movement occurs naturally. And they happen very quickly too. The prayer log and the areas set aside for artwork quickly fill up with people's prayers and inspiring chunks of Scripture. Within minutes of arriving in the room, you find yourself surrounded by all this passionate creativity, and you somehow get caught up in the 'current' … and as you pray *you* contribute to it, you take it just a little bit further. In a profound and yet subtle way, your week of prayer changes from being a 'project' to a *journey of faith* for the church community.

> *Our ten-hour stint is almost finished, and God has done so much with us tonight! We painted like madmen artists, prayed like obsessed (and extremely excited and motivated) young Christians. The power of the Holy*

Spirit is really moving and affecting our lives. We can feel him in the room, and whoever's in here after us is going to have one banging prayer session!
STEVE

Although mildly inconvenient, praying in this one room also creates a place of accountability – you *have to* turn up for the slots you've signed up for or you will (noticeably) be 'letting the side down' and breaking the non-stop chain. But turning up is no great hardship – in fact, it is probably good discipline! Each visit to the 24-7 Prayer room becomes a mini-pilgrimage, a conscious and costly journey to an ordinary place that, for you and your co-pilgrims, has somehow become a sacred space.

#2: Unity

An imaginary 24-7 Prayer room – this could easily be yours …

It is 11pm. I've been in the prayer room for the last three hours with friends from my cell group – one is a teacher, and as today's theme has been 'education' we've prayed especially for the children and staff at her school, and for her to find ways to 'live the kingdom of God' in her classroom. We've also prayed for one another, for our jobs and families and for those we are trying to reach out to. As we are gathering our coats and shoes, a group of teenagers and one of the youth workers bundle in, some with sleeping bags. They're signed in for the night and are planning to sleep and pray in shifts, one at a time. We exchange a short prayer as we pass, and symbolically I hand the prayer-log over to one of the young people – like a baton – the race is theirs now. I smile inwardly – they will run as I sleep. I wait outside for a moment and listen – the music changes, the volume rises, and I hear the sound of faith-filled, big-vision prayers. I thank God for them as I head home.

At 6am the following morning, two businessmen arrive. The air is sweet with incense (which probably hides some of the less pleasant smells), cushions are scattered across the room, and a quiet chill-out CD is playing – two of the young people are asking God to help them 'be effective for him' at school later that day. The businessmen join them, and the unlikely quartet pray for one another, exchanging words of encouragement. Minutes later, the teenagers have left and the businessmen begin their hour.

One of the men begins reading through the prayer-triggers for today's theme – the family. The other switches the CD for a more traditional worship one and glances at the prayer-log lying open on a low table, as he hums along. He flicks through the pages, reading the scrawled, passionate prayers of the teenagers' night-watch (some are still asleep in the room next door). He finds himself deeply moved by an entry expressing abandoned love for Father God, and he kneels and prays for whoever wrote it. It makes him think of his own teenage daughter, still struggling with her faith and her identity – he searches for words to make sense of his deep longing for her to find this same 'abandoned love for God', and as he does, the tears come. The other businessman notices – he brings his Bible over and reads a Scripture he's found in the day's prayer-triggers, which seems appropriate and encouraging, and then they pray together. And the peace of God comes to them both. They then begin to reach out in prayer to other families in their community.

At 7am, just before they leave, the church administrator arrives for her hour. To her surprise she meets an elderly couple at the door who aren't on the rota for that slot. They explain that they woke early that morning feeling the need to come and pray, so the three of them walk in and they greet the two businessmen. The new arrivals offer to pray that God would bless the businessmen's day. The two men both laugh, saying that they already feel that God has blessed them, but they pray together anyway. After the businessmen leave, the church administrator returns to the wall she's been painting on every day since the start of the week – a beautiful picture of a sunrise is gradually emerging – it is her prayer, her anticipation of a 'new day'. Meanwhile, the elderly couple make their way across to the opposite side of the room where people have stuck post-it notes with prayer requests from friends and neighbours and local residents (a small team from the church have been visiting local homes for the last few days, asking people 'what the church can pray for', and have gathered a surprising number of requests. Some of these people have even visited the prayer room over the last day or two, and one young mother had asked to be prayed for while she was there). During their hour, the couple pray over every single request … and so it continues.

Unity is about loving one another, being kind to one another, having our hearts turned towards (Mal. 4:6) one another, being one in spirit and truth. It doesn't mean that we have to like the same music, or even enjoy the same style of worship. Being in the same Sunday meeting doesn't unite us, any more than participating in different models and expressions of church divides us. It's a heart thing.

24-7 Prayer rooms allow unity to be expressed amongst glorious diversity. The young and the not-so-young can meet in the shared space of prayer, while remaining free to express their prayers in differing ways. Sufficiently far from the restraints of a particular church tradition, believers from different ecclesiastical backgrounds can share the common themes of the prayer room – prayer and mission and justice – without hesitation. And, as in the story above, the rich businessman in his suit and tie can stand humbly with the debt-laden student, in prayerful co-dependence.

Prayer is the great equaliser, because there are no 'great pray-ers', relatively speaking. We all come into the presence of God as equals – as children in need of our Heavenly Father, more aware of our failure than our successes, stripped of all that we thought was important and deeply grateful for God's amazing grace. Unity is easy in a place like this.

And in the shared location of the 24-7 Prayer room, you will find that pray-ers experience a strong sense of being part of a community of faith. As you pass the prayer 'baton' backwards and forwards, you are all playing your part in the team, in the 'army of ordinary people'. As one body, united.

#3: Creativity

There have been times over the past couple of years when I simply could not find the words to express what I was feeling to God (or to anyone else, for that matter). The night I sat with friends and watched *The Passion of the Christ* is one example – like countless others, I wept with shame and yet tremendous gratitude, for at least an hour after the film had ended, deeply moved by what Jesus had endured on my behalf. I felt unable to say or pray a single word, knowing that *any* word would feel utterly empty and meaningless.

There have been moments when I've felt completely overwhelmed by the incredible love of God, when I've felt transfixed, my breath taken away by God's ridiculously generous love for me. And yet there have also been moments, days and weeks even, when inexpressible sadness has suffocated me into silence. In these moments words are either impossible, or they simply aren't enough. And in those moments, I think I've experienced a little of what Scripture describes as the 'groans that words cannot express' (Rom. 8:26), where the Spirit in me has helped me pray.

I'm learning how to pray in other ways too, though – with poetry, with drawing, through writing in my journal and even (when no-one else is around to watch!) through physical movement. For me, in those moments when words are woefully inadequate, these forms have been liberating – a way to communicate with my Heavenly Father, who hears my heart through it all.

Although (with some encouraging exceptions) the church is still only just beginning to rediscover *creativity*, the many non-verbal and traditional forms are highly conducive to prayer and worship. Sculpture and dance and movement, poetry and painting, drawing and music in its many forms, all allow us to draw nearer to our Creator God.

Many people find the creativity in 24-7 Prayer rooms the most inspiring part. And the fact that the prayer room is a 'new' space, away from home, encourages them to be 'new' and creative themselves. On the 24-7 Prayer website there are pages of photos of artwork and sculpture from prayer rooms. The next chapter will suggest some practical ways to encourage *creativity* in your 24-7 Prayer room, and then the whole of the second section is full of creative ideas for use during your prayer week.

#4: Presence

As we've already agreed, the God who is everywhere is sometimes *somewhere*.

Scripture is full of examples, so is church history, and so (I'm guessing) is your personal experience. There are times and places where you have *felt* the presence of God, tangibly, and sometimes this sense of the closeness of God prevails for long periods. The Celtic Christians called these times and places 'thin places'. 'Thin places' are 'thick' with the presence of God, they are the places where the veil between heaven and earth is so thin that prayer is easier and the still, small voice of God is more clearly heard.

> *I am experiencing life with God. He is in everything I do here. I feel his presence and it's warm. I feel at ease here ... I am excited at the thought of coming here again in the week. It's also been quite strange as this evening seems timeless – each minute seems to go on forever and I'm thankful for that because the longer time goes, the longer I can stay in this room in the presence of God – and boy, is that good!*
>
> LOTTIE

Like many others before you, you will find that there are periods in your 24-7 Prayer room when God's presence is more tangibly felt. Often this comes as the momentum builds over a period of days, as prayer is sustained and the spiritual temperature rises.

#5: Mission

24-7 Prayer is about prayer and mission and justice (and probably lots of other things too). When Jesus turned away from the crowds for a moment, to tell his disciples, 'The harvest is plentiful but the workers are few. Ask the Lord of the harvest, therefore, to send out workers into his harvest field' (Mt. 9:37-38), I think he did it with a smile on his face. I think he knew very well that as soon as that obediently prayed prayer tumbled out of his disciples' mouths, that God would reply, 'Go on then! I'll send you!' In fact, the very next few verses in the NIV translation are entitled 'Jesus sends out the twelve'!

Very often as we pray, God encourages, enables and empowers us to go and become the answer to our own prayers:

> *'God, please bless so-and-so ...'*

> *'OK, I'll send you – go bless them, take them out for a meal or give them some money ... etc!'*

> *'God, please do something about homeless people.'*

> *'OK, I'll send you – give to organisations working with them, change your career, volunteer some time, learn about the causes of homelessness and get involved in helping to tackle those causes ... etc!'*

> *'God, please heal so-and-so ...'*

> *'OK, I'll send you – go and pray for them, encourage them, hug them ...'*

'God, please speak to my neighbour – they really need to know you ...'

'OK, I'll send you – if they get to know you then they'll get to know me. Go and eat with them, drink with them, pray for them and tell them about me ...'

That's the 'going' part.

But there's a 'coming' part too. Although a 24-7 Prayer room would fail miserably to meet 'seeker friendly' criteria, people who wouldn't call themselves Christians and who would probably shrink away from visiting a local church are *often* found inside a prayer room. Maybe it's the non-threatening nature of the prayer room that attracts people? Maybe it's the inspirational creativity – the sights and smells and sounds and flavours? Maybe it's the freedom just to come and sit and watch or meditate, without being asked 'Can I help you?' within seconds of arriving? Maybe it's the honesty and vulnerability of the prayers in the prayer-log, the anguish and struggle that people find resonating with their own lives? Maybe it's the space to ask quiet questions? Maybe it is simply that people feel closer to God in the prayer room?

Whatever it is, it works. People who wouldn't call themselves Christians have found their way into makeshift prayer rooms for clubbers in Ibiza, into a prayer room in someone's cellar in Sheffield, into a 24-7 Prayer Boiler Room in an old pub in Reading, and into literally hundreds of others, all over the world ... and these people have encountered God in a real way.

Lord Jesus, I can't deny it to myself any more – YOU ARE REAL! I have been searching everywhere for answers and for things that will make me happy – drugs, alcohol, dodgy relationships ... I've been there! And suddenly my eyes have been opened and now I see that what I need has been here all along. I am the kind of person who is always smiling and having a laugh, but just now I smiled FOR REAL. Because I know it's you God. Lord show me how I can trust you ...

ANON

I've been here since 11pm. When I walked in the room I felt a real desire to cry out to God for my family, friends and work colleagues. I'd done this for a while but then when I stopped I started wondering whether God had heard – whether all this prayer was really going to make a difference, it seemed such an uphill struggle.

As I was wondering, who should walk in the prayer room but my brother-in-law! His name is in our prayer room 'net'! He isn't a Christian but my sister, his wife, is. They came in together and stayed for about forty minutes – he asked lots of questions and I've just finished by praying for him! Amazing! God does hear and answer our prayers, so DON'T GIVE UP!

LIZ

There is a tremendous hunger amongst people today to rediscover holy places – places of safety and sanctuary and spirituality, places of meaning beyond the accelerated lives we lead. And as someone has said, 'Just because people don't want to be preached at doesn't mean they don't want to pray or be prayed for.'

So ... why pray in a room? – for all of these reasons, and probably many more as well. After a few days in your prayer room, you'll have your own stories to tell and reasons with which to answer that question for your own community of faith. The important thing to remember is to design your room with these things in mind – unity, continuity, creativity, presence and mission – try to design your 24-7 Prayer room in such a way that you encourage all of these.

WHERE TO LOCATE YOUR 24-7 PRAYER ROOM?

Location, location, location ... they say it is *everything*, don't they? Well, it doesn't seem to mean a *great* deal when situating a 24-7 Prayer room.

Perhaps we ought to research this a bit? From memory, I know that there have been 24-7 Prayer rooms in homes and church buildings, in schools and colleges and youth centres, in cafes and bars, in a Naval Academy, in a prison and in London's Houses of Parliament, in a caravan and on buses, in tents and towers, and (probably everyone's favourite so far) in a brewery in Missouri, and that's naming just a few.

Having reinforced how weird and wild the location of your prayer room can be, there are some practical questions or factors that you might need to consider before situating it but please don't feel daunted by these – there is *always* a way to make your prayer room work!

- *Where is it in the local community?* Is it central? This isn't essential, but you may need to think about how far you are expecting people to travel to the prayer room to fulfil their late-night slots, and whether there are sufficient transport options for people to get there and back.

- *Is it accessible?* Can the prayer room be accessed directly from the outside? This might be important during daytimes, so that the coming and going of pray-ers causes minimal disruptions to the rest of the building, and during night-times, so that the rest of it remains secure.

- *What is it close to?* If it is very close to a residential area, you will need to think about the noise of people coming and going, and of the prayer activities, i.e. do you need a curfew on the use of music in the room?

- *Is it big enough?* There is no optimum size – I have visited prayer rooms that can fit three or four people in, and others that can fit a hundred with ease. You will simply need to ask yourself if there is enough space for people, a) to feel free to pray what they want to, without worrying about other people overhearing, b) to be creative, and c) for the number of people that you're expecting at any one time (plus a few surprises)?

- *What facilities do you have?* This might sound obvious but having toilet facilities and drink-making facilities available are *essential*. You will also need to consider any health and safety or fire or child protection regulations that might affect how the prayer room functions in your building.

- *Is it secure?* You will need to think about how to keep the prayer room secure, and especially how you will manage the night hours. We always suggest that 24-7 Prayer rooms think this through carefully, and at the very least, ensure that there is a land-line or mobile available in the room at all times and a list of emergency numbers to call.

HOW DOES IT WORK? HOW CAN YOU FILL 168 HOURS WITH PRAYER?

Most groups or churches find filling the slots easier than they expect. Once people have completed their first promised hour of prayer (which they may have only agreed to because you arm-twisted them into signing up!), they discover that they love being in the 24-7 Prayer room, and so they come back for more.

Having said this, *some* groups or churches initially feel that it is unrealistic to fill the whole 24x7, 168 hours with prayer. Chapter 6 will explore some alternative ways for you to host a week of prayer *without* praying 24-7, but here are a few ideas that might help you manage it;

- Invite another group or church to join with you in attempting to fill the full 24-7 Prayer week – this is a good exercise in unity in itself.

- Give each small group the responsibility to fill a 24-hour period – maybe the leadership team could take one too?

- Invite youth groups or small groups to take on the night-watches, i.e. have them sleep over in a nearby room and take turns praying in the prayer room throughout the night.

- If the 24-7 Prayer week seems unrealistic because you have so many other church activities going on, then consider closing them down for a week and focusing your effort and energies on prayer. If it is because a bunch of your most committed people are away, then consider shifting the whole week to more convenient dates.

Once you have agreed on dates and a venue, once you've got your leaders on board and a team is beginning to form, and you're starting to communicate the vision and the practicalities to your group or church, then it's time to draw up your rota – a bit like the one below but *much* bigger. It needs to be *huge* – big enough to see from a distance, for people to be able to sign their names onto, and for you to be able to add things to.

When I draw up a 24-7 Prayer week rota, I tend to stick a couple of lengths of lining paper together, which leaves me with something about as long and as wide as a king-sized bed. This might sound enormous (it is!) but it allows lots of people to gather around it and discuss where they're going to sign up.

The rota

Sun	Mon	Tues	Wed	Thurs	Fri	Sat	Sun
	Mid-1am	Mid-1am	Mid-1am	Mid-1am	Mid-1am	Mid-1am	Mid-1am
	1am-2am	1am-2am	1am-2am	1am-2am	1am-2am	1am-2am	1am-2am
	2am-3am	2am-3am	2am-3am	2am-3am	2am-3am	2am-3am	2am-3am
	3am-4am	3am-4am	3am-4am	3am-4am	3am-4am	3am-4am	3am-4am
	4am-5am	4am-5am	4am-5am	4am-5am	4am-5am	4am-5am	4am-5am
	5am-6am	5am-6am	5am-6am	5am-6am	5am-6am	5am-6am	5am-6am
	6am-7am	6am-7am	6am-7am	6am-7am	6am-7am	6am-7am	6am-7am
	7am-8am	7am-8am	7am-8am	7am-8am	7am-8am	7am-8am	7am-8am
	8am-9am	8am-9am	8am-9am	8am-9am	8am-9am	8am-9am	8am-9am
	9am-10am	9am-10am	9am-10am	9am-10am	9am-10am	9am-10am	9am-10am
	10am-11am	10am-11am	10am-11am	10am-11am	10am-11am	10am-11am	10am-11am
	11am-12mid	11am-12mid	11am-12mid	11am-12mid	11am-12mid	11am-12mid	11am-12mid
12mid-1pm	12mid-1pm	12mid-1pm	12mid-1pm	12mid-1pm	12mid-1pm	12mid-1pm	
1pm-2pm	1pm-2pm	1pm-2pm	1pm-2pm	1pm-2pm	1pm-2pm	1pm-2pm	
2pm-3pm	2pm-3pm	2pm-3pm	2pm-3pm	2pm-3pm	2pm-3pm	2pm-3pm	
3pm-4pm	3pm-4pm	3pm-4pm	3pm-4pm	3pm-4pm	3pm-4pm	3pm-4pm	
4pm-5pm	4pm-5pm	4pm-5pm	4pm-5pm	4pm-5pm	4pm-5pm	4pm-5pm	
5pm-6pm	5pm-6pm	5pm-6pm	5pm-6pm	5pm-6pm	5pm-6pm	5pm-6pm	
6pm-7pm	6pm-7pm	6pm-7pm	6pm-7pm	6pm-7pm	6pm-7pm	6pm-7pm	
7pm-8pm	7pm-8pm	7pm-8pm	7pm-8pm	7pm-8pm	7pm-8pm	7pm-8pm	
8pm-9pm	8pm-9pm	8pm-9pm	8pm-9pm	8pm-9pm	8pm-9pm	8pm-9pm	
9pm-10pm	9pm-10pm	9pm-10pm	9pm-10pm	9pm-10pm	9pm-10pm	9pm-10pm	
10pm-11pm	10pm-11pm	10pm-11pm	10pm-11pm	10pm-11pm	10pm-11pm	10pm-11pm	
11pm-mid	11pm-mid	11pm-mid	11pm-mid	11pm-mid	11pm-mid	11pm-mid	

Note: *Most 24-7 Prayer weeks have started and finished at 8pm on Sunday evenings, to coincide with evening meetings/events, which are good for launching and closing ceremonies. You can change this as appropriate.*

As already mentioned, you could block out the first two hours (12midday-2pm Sunday) as some kind of launching ceremony, and the final two hours (10am-12midday second Sunday) as a story-telling closing ceremony. You could also block out certain slots as worship times, during which you could invite someone to lead worship for an hour or so. A prayer room I visited last year had an early morning guided session every day – it lasted about an hour, was led by a different person each morning and drew on various traditional liturgies. A lot of people attended these prayer hours.

Having done this, your task is to persuade others to sign up for slots and get the rota filled. You could encourage people to come and pray alone, or to come with partners or close friends, or even to come with their whole small group. Do encourage everyone to make the most of it.

A recent advert I saw on the London Underground read something like this: 'There are 168 hours in your week – do something useful with eight of them.' The huge poster then invited readers to become a Special Constable and to volunteer eight hours of their week to this role. Although it sounds like a lot, I've been encouraging people to use this as a target for the week – to aim to spend eight hours in the prayer room over the seven days.

Eight hours in a prayer room might demand some readjustment, but surely that's ok? If all we do is 'fit' prayer into our already busy lifestyles, then we've missed the point. David once said, 'I will not … sacrifice a burnt offering that costs me nothing' (1 Chr. 21:24). Maybe it needs to cost us? You could encourage people to fast as well – maybe, instead of fasting food, you could all fast television for the duration of the week (I would recommend this), and then spend the same amount of time that you would have been watching television in the prayer room instead?

> *Me (Sarah), Sam and Jody are going to fast for a year. For three months we are not going to have chocolate. For two months we are fasting fizzy drinks … and we don't know what the others things are going to be yet. Maybe be a vegetarian for a month? Also not to argue for a month. We will also save our money and give it to charity. Please pray for us.*
>
> SARAH, SAM AND JODY (12)

The final thing to say about the rota is this – you will need to recruit a small team of 'on-call' people, ideally one for each 24-hour period (maybe midday till midday). Their role, during their 24-hour period is to:

• Make sure that every slot is filled – if there are empty slots, they need to do some 'friendly phoning' and get them filled, or pray themselves).

- Make sure that the prayer room is reasonably tidy – which will probably mean a visit later in their day as well).
- Make sure that supplies of coffee, milk, tea, etc. are restocked.
- Be available on a mobile phone for any emergency calls. Their number will need to be available in the prayer room and they will need to be ready to go to the prayer room immediately if needed, day or night.

WHO IS 24-7 PRAYER FOR?

Some people still seem to think that 24-7 Prayer is a 'youth' thing. It's not. If you visit 24-7 Prayer rooms across the UK you will find children and young people, those who are 'middle-aged' (whatever that is) and those at the further end of the age-continuum … you will find Methodist and Salvationists, Catholics and charismatics, Anglicans and agnostics, black and white, women and men, the very wealthy and the poor and homeless. And then if you went visiting beyond the UK, you would find an *even greater* diversity. So, 24-7 Prayer includes everyone. All are welcome!

Having said that, maybe because of the perceived 'extreme' nature of early-hours praying, 24-7 Prayer rooms do seem to attract young people. If this happens, let them loose. Let them lead the way in passionate prayer. And the children too – if you do what we do and encourage people to paint their prayers onto the walls (some prayer room organisers prefer just to hang sheets, or stick paper up), then you will find many children want to join in!

WHAT DO WE NEED IN THE PRAYER ROOM?

In addition to all the creative stuff that we'll look at in the next chapter, here's a checklist of practical things that you will probably want to have available in your 24-7 Prayer room:

- Coffee and tea-making facilities – kettle, cups, milk, biscuits, sugar, spoons, coffee, tea and hot chocolate, etc.
- A CD-player and some CDs – a variety of worship, chill-out and dance/trance compilations – people often bring their own.
- The rota, prominently displayed.
- A PC or laptop with access to the www.24-7prayer.com website. Not many groups or churches are able to do this, but it can provide lots of good triggers for prayer during the week, and a place to receive encouragement from others. If you *do* have a PC or laptop, you will probably need to produce a simple 'instruction sheet' and some 'PC-use rules' as well.

- Basic stationery stuff – sellotape, paper, pens, pencils, Blu-Tack, scissors, paints and brushes, drawing pins, other art materials.
- A prayer-log.
- Incense and scented candles.
- Regular candles or other small lamps – Christmas tree lights are great!
- A notice-board with important information – security details, on-call mobile number, rules of the room, directions to facilities/toilets, etc.

This has been a long chapter, and lots of it has been *information* rather than *inspiration*, so you might be feeling a little bit 'fried' at this stage. Don't worry! If any of this is confusing, or if it has triggered lots of questions that you can't find answers to elsewhere in this book, then you can try these options:

- Check the *24-7 Prayer Manual*, which describes more fully how to set up a 24-7 Prayer room
- Email 24-7 Prayer with your questions – uk@24-7prayer.com

We'll do our best to help you make your 24-7 Prayer week a milestone moment.

[4] Douglas Coupland, *Life after God*, (London: Scribner, 2002)

5 CREATIVE PRAYING
- MORE THAN 'HANDS TOGETHER AND EYES CLOSED'

Our prayer room is painted white and softly lit, and in the corner we have a tent. The smell of incense fills the room – it really is amazing. I can hear Delirious' "Come Like You Promise" playing from another corner. I've just spent 45 minutes in our tent. It's a really tiny tent and as soon as you get in, the feeling of security is there. I'm not sure how to put it but God really met me. As I chatted and sang, those reassuring Holy Spirit feelings came. You know, the tingling down your spine. I could vividly imagine God smiling over me and I just felt good in his presence – not condemned but welcome.

PETE

A couple of years ago someone said to me, 'It's time for you to get out of the garden, and get into the field.' I felt it was a word from God, and so did my friends – a word about being free and wild, a word about movement and journey, a word about discovering new things and rediscovering ancient, well-trodden paths that have since become overgrown – and I still feel the relevance of this word on and in my life.

Although a lot of planning goes into a 24-7 Prayer room (as you are about to find out!), it is, or it becomes, a wild place, a place of freedom and discovery and a place of journey. What might start out as a well-tended garden quickly becomes a messy field of overgrowing prayer and worship. Yet, even in the messiness, paths and patterns begin to emerge – we begin to hear God speaking in and over and through it all. And some of these tracks will lead you into your local community in surprising ways.

There are probably lots of reasons why people find they can express their thoughts and feelings to God more creatively in a 24-7 Prayer room. We've already explored some – the lack of words to say or pray sometimes, the inspiration of others' creative expressions (creativity always begets more creativity) – and here are a few others

- The *space* and *artistic materials* – sitting alone in a prayer room with a paint palette in front of you, in front of a blank wall, is very inviting,

- The *time* – the busyness of life often prevents us from pausing to think or reflect much at all. In Carl Honoré's brilliant book, *In Praise of Slow*, he urges readers to 'make time for activities that defy acceleration'. A 24-7 Prayer room is one of these activities … and, liberated briefly from the pressure of to-do lists and responsibilities, we find our imaginations free. We are free to create.

A liberated imagination is a prerequisite for facing the future.[5]

- The *lack of a structure or programme* – an hour (or two) in a 24-7 Prayer room can be very different to an hour (or two) in a regular prayer meeting. There generally is no particular programme or liturgy to follow, and there usually is no one leading or guiding the time – there's just you, or you and a few others, in a room full of sights and sounds and smells, things to touch and things to do something with or about. But it's a safe place, and it's an exciting place, pregnant with something (or Someone) waiting to happen. Some people find the freedom intimidating at first, so try to help them find a place where they feel comfortable to start (such as a prayer-log – the book of your group or church community's prayers), and then stretch out from there.

- Almost in contrast, because of its inclusiveness, a 24-7 Prayer room *welcomes* and embraces a wide variety of prayer liturgy and church tradition. 24-7 Prayer rooms have appeared in incredibly diverse church traditions, and ecumenical (multi-denominational) prayer rooms have been hosted successfully in many different places. As these traditions and their accompanying liturgies are brought together, with generosity and mutual humility, a glorious fusion begins to take place. There is much that we can learn from one another and from God through this.

In Part 2 you will find an assortment of great ideas and triggers for creative praying, all centred around particular themes. Our hope is that these launch you from prayer into action, from praying into becoming the answer to many of your prayers, from intimacy into involvement in your many communities. And you might like to check out the *world around you*! Before you go any further, why don't you put this book down for a moment and just look around the place you're in right now – what objects could you take into a 24-7 Prayer room that could inspire or encourage prayer? Take a few minutes – you'll be surprised at what you come up with … and then there's a whole world out there!

PRAY CONTINUALLY

24-7 currently have an office situated near to St Paul's Cathedral in central London. High in the dome of the Cathedral is a place called the Whispering Gallery, where a whisper can travel from one side of the dome around to the other with surprising clarity. I remember visiting when I was young, resting my ear on the stone wall and marvelling at my sister's whispers as they crept smoothly around the walls for a few seconds.

Someone once told me that sound never actually disappears. The sound waves created by our words and music, even our whispers, continue forever, decreasing but never disappearing. James encourages (and warns) his readers to make sure that our words are full of goodness and praise, like fresh water (Jas. 3:1-12). In 24-

7 Prayer rooms our prayers, spoken or sung or played on instruments, disappear beyond our audible range within a few seconds, but heaven reverberates with them forever.

Although these audible prayers leave us in a moment, our written prayers – our poetry and prose and letters to God, scribbled into the prayer-log and painted onto 'or scratched into?' the walls – as well as our sculptures and our prophetic symbols – remain. They remain, not only for the eyes of heaven, but for others who share that place of prayer. These physical prayers, although no more important than our audible prayers, have a lasting impact and they continue to move, inspire and challenge others who participate in the prayer room. Pray continually.

There really are very few, if any, rules when it comes to prayer and to creativity in general, only principles. When setting up your 24-7 Prayer room, you will want to simply create a space that glorifies God, and enables people to encounter God, whether they have done so before or not.

Why not gather some of the creative people in your group or church and commission them to kit out the room? Give them this book, a small budget and a list of the essential elements and principles (and make sure that they know that the room is *for others to use*, not a showcase for them … just in case), and then leave them to create something wonderful. Two final tips:

1 Don't fill your prayer room up with loads of stuff. Leave quite a lot of space for people to fit in and to move around.

2 Don't turn your prayer room into a masterpiece before anyone has even visited it. Leave a bit of mess so that people don't feel intimidated and reluctant to be creative for fear that *they* will mess it up.

CRAZY PRAYING

Here are a few examples of creative ideas and elements in 24-7 Prayer rooms I've been involved in:

- *Tubs of paints and pens and lots of paper*. My daughters, Megan (7) and Poppy (5), love 24-7 Prayer rooms because they are free to paint and draw. They might not be able to compose an eloquent verbal prayer like the adults in the room, but they can express how they feel with a paintbrush or a crayon as well as anyone. And they've learnt about prayer through watching others paint and draw and create and write. Most children are naturally creative, so set them free to be.

- *Local area information*. It's good to have some visual triggers from your local area, if that's a focus for your prayer. Maps are good and so are local newspapers. I visited an extraordinary 24-7 Prayer room (in fact, it was five rooms, each with a separate theme and style) in Thurrock recently. In a large room they'd draped a long blue cloth from one end to the other in the shape of the River Thames and had marked key points and buildings all the way along. Inspired by this, I soon found myself 'wading' barefoot up and down the 'river', praying all kinds of things for our capital city.

- *Photo board.* In a recent prayer room, we invited everyone to bring a small photo of themselves and pin it onto a large noticeboard. As the week went by, others wrote prayers and words of encouragement onto post-it notes and stuck them near to the photos. It was a wonderful exercise in loving and encouraging one another.

- *Comfortable space.* Most 24-7 Prayer rooms have a corner or an area with cushions or bean-bags or small sofas and soft lighting for people to relax and pray, by themselves or with one another. In a prayer room I helped to co-ordinate we also had a tiny tent to curl up in, representing the tabernacle of God or the 'holy of holies'. Another time we created a kind of cave to crawl into. I spent a couple of hours in our cave one night and God spoke to me about listening for his still, small voice amongst all the noise in my life.

- *Music.* This is probably obvious, but make sure you have a working CD player with a variety of CDs available for use in prayer and worship. We've also tried to make sure that there are a few small instruments available – small drums, a guitar, sticks to bash with, etc. You could arrange for someone to lead an hour of worship each day at a set time, maybe even someone from a different church tradition.

- *The Internet.* Although this is difficult for some groups or churches to set up, having access to the www.24-7prayer.com website throughout the week is really useful. During one of our early 24-7 Prayer rooms, people started to post their prayers, their thoughts and their answers to prayer onto the 24-7 Prayer website discussion boards, which are available for anyone in the world to read. As the week went by, Christians from all over the world began to send emails and post responses onto what we'd posted – the sense of global partnership in prayer was very exciting.

- *Prophetic symbols.* I've been in 24-7 Prayer rooms where people have brought a bowl of water to wash in, a symbol of forgiveness and cleanliness; a box to put shoes in, a response to the Scripture, 'Take off your sandals, for the place where you are standing is holy' (Josh. 5:15); a 'sin bin' to throw items or confessions into – (this was taken outside and burnt later in the week) a symbol of freedom from sin; a bucket of stones, symbols of the small smooth stones that David used to kill Goliath, and of the stones that are frequently 'set up' in the Old Testament to mark certain moments and encounters with God. There are many more examples and you will probably have some soon.

- *Mission and Fishing.* In one prayer room, someone had hung a large fishing net from the ceiling and had cut out lots of paper fish. During the week, as people prayed for their friends and family, neighbours and work colleagues, they wrote their names onto the fish and threw them into the net. During another week of 24-7 Prayer, the net was hung down a wall and people used clothes pegs to attached their prayers to it.

- *Prayer-log.* In every 24-7 Prayer room, we've had an A4 sized, plain-paged book, decorated by someone with a bit of creative flair, and set on a small table in the room. We've encouraged pray-ers to sometimes write their prayers in there, to draw, to add Scriptures they feel inspired by, to describe their dreams, visions and pictures, to record any words from God and to tell their stories. Over the course of the week this log becomes a communal story, a record of our journey together. Patterns frequently emerge and together we begin to discern what God might be saying to our group or church community. It also serves as a place for people who aren't in the prayer room at the same time to interact.

One of the local leaders was reading the prayer-log and found a page full of scratchy red writing. It caught her eye and she started to read it. It had been written (anonymously) by a young girl, admitting for the first time to the abuse and sadness in her life. She'd written it all in the log because, as she said, 'I feel safe here.' The leader stuck a post-it to the page – 'Well done for being so brave,' she wrote. 'If you want to talk and pray, I'll be here at these times …' A few days later the leader discovered a post-it reply from the young girl, saying that she wanted to talk – she felt it was time to do so, but she still felt scared. The leader left a second post-it note, giving her contact details, praying that the girl would make contact. She didn't. Their 24-7 Prayer week ended without any further post-its …

The next week, in her small youth cell group, the leader explained what had happened and her concern for this girl. When she'd finished, they all began to pray, they cried out to God for grace and healing and somehow for the young girl to make contact again. As the praying subsided, a voice from the corner whispered … 'It was me. I wrote it. It's me.'

The leader and girl's friends in the cell gathered around her, hugged her and prayed for her, soaking her with love and grace. And healing began.

So, make space for creative prayer. Encourage it. Encourage people who are used to *verbal* prayer to experiment with other ways and forms, to find other ways to express their love for Jesus. (I try to do this with my wife, so why not with Jesus?)

Be sensitive to one another. Be open to new (and older!) traditions, and expect to hear from God and discover new things about yourself. And use your imagination. God did, and the universe came into being.

[5] Brian Walsh and Richard Middleton, *Truth is Stranger than it used to be* (London: SPCK, 1995)

Prayerworks: Part 1

6 ALTERNATIVES TO A WEEK OF 24-7 PRAYER

For I have the desire to do what is good, but I cannot carry it out. (Rom. 7:18b)

A 24-7 Prayer room is 'good' for lots of reasons – it is good for individuals, for local groups or churches, and for whole networks: it is good for mission, creativity, unity, continuity and for encountering the presence of God (and probably for much more) – but you may genuinely feel that you 'cannot carry it out.' Although a 24-7 Prayer room is a very simple model, it requires a lot of effort, energy and commitment. We've already considered Lyndall Bywater's wise advice, 'Where possible, we very strongly urged people to stick to the 'normal' idea (168 hours of non-stop prayer in one room) … (but) prayer is the key thing, and as much of it as possible …'

If you've come this far and you really love the idea of setting up a prayer room, but, having talked with your local leadership, you genuinely don't feel that your group or church can carry it out yet, for whatever reason, here's some alternative ways to host a week of prayer. And I did say 'yet' for a reason – don't give up on the dream of setting up a 24-7 Prayer room if it's not immediately realistic. A time will come, and probably sooner than you think.

Before you settle for one of these options, do have a careful check back through the paragraph in Chapter 4 where I suggested some additional ways to make a 24-7 Prayer week *work*. Wherever possible, try to do it.

ALTERNATIVES …

- Do a 24-2 prayer room. Set up your prayer room in the way we've explored so far and pray from midday Friday until midday Sunday (Pentecost Sunday, if that's when you are hosting your week).

- Or even just do a 24-1, praying from midday Saturday until midday Sunday.

- If the night-times are a problem because of security, etc., do a daylight/office-hours prayer room, maybe 9am – 5pm each day and different times at the weekend.

- Alternatively, if the night-times are the easier part, do a night of prayer, or even a few of them, maybe Thursday, Friday and Saturday nights, 8pm-2am or whatever suits you.

- Do a morning and evening 'daily prayers' style prayer room, maybe from 6am-8am in the morning and 8pm-10pm in the evening. You could make a few of them slightly earlier in the evening and set them up more for children.

- Or you could do just mornings or just evenings. Be aware, however, that if your prayer room, whether it's in a church building or someone's home, is only open for short periods (two to three hours), the prayer room can become a prayer meeting in the minds of those participating. If so, those participating will probably expect someone to be leading it from start to finish, telling them what to pray, when to pray, how to pray and where to pray. Try to avoid doing this from the front if you can – only give guidance and direction where it is really necessary and remember that it can be given through the layout of a room as much as through words from the front.

- If your group or church is spread out across an area, then spread out the prayer room, maybe with one day in a home in each locality, hosted by someone locally. The 24-7 Prayer week in Parliament was a bit like this, in that the 'prayer room' moved from offices to meeting rooms to chapels throughout the week – what helped to make it work was

  - still encouraging people to sign up for certain time-slots

  - having someone responsible for each new location

  - having a prayer-log that got carried from location to location

  Together these helped to retain a sense of meaningful continuity.

- If your group or church really do find the lack of guidance from the front in the prayer room uncomfortable, you could slot in some guided sessions or even parts of sessions. If you are hosting an open 24-7 Prayer room it's always worth having a few designated explainers for visitors who arrive and wonder what on earth is going on. During a night of prayer, for example, you could start with a short introduction, using content from Part 2 of this book, for ten minutes, and then encourage people to spread around the room and make use of the various resources to express their prayers or to talk with God. You could then gather them back again to start the next hour and each subsequent hour.

Do feel free to mix and match the suggestions listed above, and if they don't work then feel free to come up with your own solutions to your particular obstacles. If you have any questions about how to set up a 24-7 Prayer room or a variation of one that this book hasn't already answered then please email us on uk@24-7prayer.com or phone us. Our telephone details can be found on the www.24-7prayer.com website.

... SEE YOU IN A PRAYER ROOM?

As I've been writing these chapters I've been flicking through prayer-logs from the different 24-7 Prayer rooms that I've had the privilege of participating in, and I've found myself deeply moved.

Jesus, heal the hurt within me Lord. Please be the dad I never had.

ANON

Reading the pages and pages of painfully honest prayer – some overflowing with hope and joy, and some revealing brokenness beyond words – I've found myself longing for time alone with my Father in a prayer room again. I've found myself recalling memories that are infused with thrill and anticipation, like my first night-time slot. At about 3am one February morning, I left the frosty air outside and crept into a cosy 24-7 Prayer room. I closed the door behind me, and just knew that I was about to embark on an adventure in prayer with my Father that I was wholly unprepared for.

As I rest on my knees at his feet, the air dense with his Spirit, I try to breathe deeper and deeper, absorbing as much of his presence as humanly possible. Lord give me the strength and don't let me forget who and what I've found in this spiritual place.

ANON

But enough of memories. It's your turn now – you and many, many others like you, in fact. I hope that you feel inspired and as prepared as you can be for the adventure ahead.

The next section is an extensive menu of resources, ideas and triggers for prayer, all wrapped around six community-related themes. Our hope is that this menu will provide you and your group or church with enough to get your 24-7 Prayer week started well. Note – these are triggers and starting points, not a comprehensive list of all you will ever need to pray about. After that, you'll find suggestions for how this short season of prayer and intimacy might unfold into greater involvement in your local communities. Prayer and mission. Prayer and action. Pray and go.

Before you move onto those stages, however, there's one final thing to explain – registering your prayer room.

REGISTERING YOUR 24-7 PRAYER ROOM

We encourage all 24-7 Prayer rooms to register on the www.24-7prayer.com website (or, for those without an Internet connection, by telephoning the 24-7 Prayer UK office). The website registration process is straightforward – it asks for your basic details and then invites you to enter the dates that your group or church are praying and finally it offers you a further selection of 24-7 Prayer resources. Once the process is complete, your group or church will appear in the on-line diary section of the website, and when your week arrives, it will also appear on the main page, listed alongside all of the other groups/churches who are praying at the same time as you, all over the world.

In the 24-7 Prayer UK office we make personal contact with *every* prayer room that registers, which is another good reason for taking those few minutes to go through the process! We telephone the co-ordinators of each prayer room before, during and after their week, partly to offer support and encouragement, partly to answer any last minute questions, and partly to exchange stories. As I've already mentioned, we've been gathering some *astonishing* stories from individual prayer rooms across the UK and then we've been sending them back out in a regular UK Report email. Whoever registers your 24-7 Prayer room will automatically receive this report.

It doesn't take a degree in 'discerning the signs of the times' to conclude that God is at work in the UK right now, in quite remarkable ways. 24-7 Prayer is *only one* of many wonderful movements and places where God's fingerprints can be found, and yet we're overwhelmed by what he's doing through this little movement alone! We're hearing of increasing numbers of networks and denominations considering following the Salvation Army's lead, and praying non-stop for a whole year, including the Methodist Church. We've been involved with 24-7 Prayer weeks in the Houses of Parliament and Whitehall. We're attempting to encourage people who are 'dreaming and scheming' about establishing Boiler Rooms in countless towns and cities across the UK (including in the City of London itself). And there's so much more than this. We are convinced that there is a 'wave' of prayer building in the UK, and at some stage it will crest and turn and crash back onto the shores of our land. And for that, we cry, 'Come on!'

> *… if my people, who are called by my name, will humble themselves and pray and seek my face and turn from their wicked ways, then will I hear from Heaven and will forgive their sin and will heal their land.*

(2 Chronicles 7:14)

Phil Togwell

PART 2:

IDEAS AND RESOURCES FOR YOUR PRAYER WEEK

Introduction

Launch event:
A sermon to start your Prayer Week

Ideas and Resources on six community themes:

Finale event

INTRODUCTION

This part of *Prayerworks* is a 'menu' of ideas and resources designed to help you plan your prayer week in the most creative, dynamic and integrated way possible.

Your 'appetiser' is a launch service sermon for the start of any Faithworks and 24/7 week of prayer for community engagement, one of two specially written by Steve Chalke. It's based around one of the ideas that's central to this book, that intimacy and involvement go hand in hand.

The 'main menu' has no less than six different community themes for your prayer week, each with its own choice selection of biblical starting points, creative prayer ideas, true stories, activities, poems, meditations and contact points. The six themes are: family; education; health, leisure and well-being; business and employment; politics, law and order, and the excluded. Use and develop any theme once you've thought about your local or church situation, remembering that the key is to blend intimacy with involvement, church with wider community, and prayer with mission.

Browsing through this section, you'll find a wide variety of ideas. Some of them lend themselves to decorating your prayer room itself. Others are more suitable for a structured lunchtime series or a one-off prayer event during your week. 'The Bible on…' bits might be good prompts for a teaching series in homegroups, before you get going with 24-7 Prayer at all. The intimacy and involvement stories are really case studies that could be read aloud or stuck on a prayer room wall as an encouragement. Several ideas, such as the group meditations, contacting community leaders or outdoor prayer activities require more advance planning than the rest. A number of the creative prayer ideas are open-ended triggers based on pop songs, TV programme or films – it's up to you how you choose these clips, lyrics and music to stimulate prayer. (Always remember the practicalities of cueing up videos or songs to the right place ahead of time, being careful not to offend anyone and so on.) The Get Connected contacts list at the end of each theme provides a number of organisations that both Faithworks and 24-7 Prayer know well and/or work with – but no doubt there are many others like them too.

Larger or more ambitious groups doing *Prayerworks* could explore a different community theme each day of the week; there are six in all, which makes a perfect fit to fill the days between your launch event and your commissioning event.

And for 'dessert' … we have a sumptuous closing service, to commission your church for local community engagement at the end of your prayer week. This sermon is based on the Pentecost account – the story of those disciples' prayers in the upper room, waiting on that avalanche of God's presence and power, which led on to mission on an unprecedented level.

PUBLIC HEALTH WARNING!

Just as you or I would be a fool to order every item off a restaurant menu, so the worst thing to do with this section would be to attempt everything. You can try, but don't hold us responsible for the results. You have been warned! Instead, be selective, bearing in mind the unique characteristics of your own church and community. Tailor your prayer week to your people in your location. This will make the week easier to run, and it will be easier for your church and your team of pray-ers and co-ordinators to own it.

For example:

- If your church is next to a school, why not run the whole prayer week on the theme of education, with a prayer box in the school to supply requests to your prayer room?

- If you have lawyers, local councillors, policemen or an MP in your congregation, explore the theme of politics, law and order and invite those church members to tell their stories at a lunchtime event.

- If your church is working with other churches locally, you could take a different idea or theme for each day of your prayer week, from Monday to Saturday.

- Why not have a small board or area in your prayer room that takes a different community theme each day, with specialists in those areas from your congregation each creating a display for 24 hours?

- How about running two or three evening events on different themes, to which you invite various community leaders and pray for them?

- Or you could organise a family fun day in your local area, with prayer built into the day at different points.

Whatever you decide to do, here is a prayer that might help as you plan:

Dear Lord, we haven't really got a clue about what's best, but we know you do. Please show us how best to run our prayer week. Save us both from complete apathy and from a 'must-do-everything' mentality. All of us in [name of church/group] want to be transformed from the inside-out and to make a difference just where you've placed us. Help us to be passionate, prayerful and 'real'. In Jesus' name … Amen.

Finally, we'd all love to hear your stories about how your prayer week goes – and what springs from it. Email your stories to info@faithworks.info or info@24-7prayer.com. Alternatively, you can post them on the 24-7 Talkback section of the www.24-7prayer.com website.

LAUNCH EVENT

A service theme to start your prayer week

Your launch event is a great reason to fill up balloons, get those party poppers out, organise a live ten second countdown, invite some experienced 24-7 Prayer people to enthuse people taking part for the first time and so on. Do all this well and it will almost certainly encourage a late rush of people signing up for those prayer slots.

This is a key moment to reiterate some of the stories and principles you've been drip feeding into the hearts and minds of your church friends for (hopefully) some weeks, and to renew both your expectation and commitment levels for the 24-7 Prayer week ahead. We recommend that the sermon below forms an integral component of your launch, as it sets the tone for prayer that is locally engaged.

INTIMACY AND INVOLVEMENT

Written by Steve Chalke, based on Matthew 22:37-39

'Your God has had plenty to say to the church in the last few decades, but very little, if anything at all, to say to the nation as a whole,' commented an agnostic writer from one of the national broadsheets. 'He's got a serious case of verbal diarrhoea when it comes to caring for his "flock". He just can't stop complimenting them. They are eagles soaring in blue skies, fruitful trees planted by free-flowing rivers and mighty warriors anointed for battle. But when it comes to the rest of society he's been struck dumb. He's either lost his nerve, lost his interest, or both.'

John 3:16 makes it clear that God loves not only the church but also the world. We don't have to look any further than Jesus himself to discover God's response is for society at large. In Matthew 22:37-39, Jesus provides us with the foundational statement for genuine Christian spirituality and orthodoxy: 'Love God with all your heart and with all your soul and with all your mind … and love your neighbour as yourself.' And what is more, these two are inextricably connected. The ability to love our neighbour the way we love ourselves is funded by loving God. Likewise, our love for God is authenticated by loving our neighbour. Or, to put it another way – intimacy with God and involvement with others are at the heart of genuine Christian faith, dynamic spirituality and a Jesus-centred lifestyle.

INTIMACY WITHOUT INVOLVEMENT

Intimacy without involvement results in irrelevance. It was Karl Marx who famously stated: 'Religion is the opiate of the masses.' It anaesthetises people and takes them inside themselves, he claimed. Another famous leader, Winston Churchill, once commented that it was always wise to 'listen to your best friends and your worst enemies … they both have something to teach you.' Instead of rejecting Marx's comment out of hand, we do well to stop long enough to reflect on it. Especially as the most dangerous characteristic of irrelevancy is that it is, more often than not, unconscious!

Who can deny that for much of the twentieth century, for instance, here in the UK, there was a tendency on the part of many churches to deal with the increasing secularisation of society by retreat? Ghetto-life was seen as the best form of defence against ungodly or worldly culture. This withdrawal into gated, spiritual communities was only punctuated by sporadic sorties out into a godless society to 'bring the lost into the fold'. But tragically, as we know, this otherworldly retreat from contamination also proved to be a long march into irrelevancy. Jesus calls us to be in but not of the world – a stance that is only possible when our intimacy with him is matched by our involvement in our communities.

INVOLVEMENT WITHOUT INTIMACY

If intimacy with God without involvement in our communities results in irrelevance, involvement in community without intimacy with God is ineffective. At the same time as some sections of the Church were on the retreat others, unimpressed with this negative, head in the sand, holy-huddle mentality, reacted to it and the pressure of their surrounding culture by throwing themselves with all their energy and commitment into politics and social engagement. Rather than saving souls, their eyes became firmly set on shaping society. Activism, not otherworldliness, was what was needed. However, unfortunately, in the desperate search to fit the prevailing secular culture, many slowly lost their Christian distinctiveness and genuine spirituality.

Involvement without intimacy leaves the church empty-handed. The reason is simple. Our task is not to bring justice, compassion or mercy to our communities, it is to bring God to them. When we do that we will also bring justice, compassion and mercy. But we can't bring a God whom we don't know. The greater the depth of our intimacy with him, the more meaningful our mission becomes.

And it is more than that: involvement without intimacy is a backbreaking and draining experience which will, in the end, leave even the greatest enthusiast dry and burnt out.

INTIMACY AND INVOLVEMENT

Only intimacy and involvement lead to real impact. Only then will we be distinctively Christian. The truth is that to subscribe to either the otherworldly notion of Christian spirituality which is all about the inner life, or alternatively to opt for the activist public service option, is to abandon truly biblically rooted Christian spirituality entirely. Spirituality that is solely focused on the inner life is no more than a crutch for the weak. But likewise, mission, activism and public service that become detached from an inner spirituality are not only backbreaking but ultimately prove to be bankrupt of the transformational power and energy of Christ.

In the words of author Mike Riddell, 'That which we claim to be aware of in our souls must become visible before it is credible. Likewise, our actions need to spring from the depths of our spirit if they are to be of substance and significance.'

Whenever spirituality and mission; prayer and action; our relationship with God and our commitment to our community become separated, history shows us that we will become either isolated from, or seduced by, our culture. But either way, our faith becomes impotent and sterile; genuine Christian spirituality is lost and the light that should be shining in the darkness is extinguished.

Jesus' teaching flies in the face of both of these mistakes. It contradicts the sacred/secular divide and calls for intimacy and involvement, a depth of spirituality and a commitment to mission, to function in harmony with one another. In fact, neither the Old or New Testament recognises any distinction between the concept of faith and the practice of faithfulness i.e., obedient activity. Biblically, no separation exists between the inner and outer life; they are two sides of the same coin. To talk about inner *versus* outer life, religion versus politics, or intercessors *versus* activists, is to attempt to drive a wedge between that which is unified by nature, turning our backs on the teaching of both the Old and New Testaments and specifically Jesus himself.

To put it as bluntly as Jesus' brother James did, 'faith by itself, if it is not accompanied by action, is dead', (Jas. 2:17). Authentic Christian faith requires us to be with God for other people, and with other people for God.

Even the word religion has its roots in the Latin word meaning reconnection. In calling us to 'Love God with all our heart and with all our soul and with all our mind … and to love our neighbour as ourselves,' Jesus calls us to reconnection with God and others. Intimacy with God and involvement with others is *true religion*.

Over the coming week we are going to be expressing our commitment to the principle of intimacy and involvement through our week of 24/7 Prayer for our community. This will culminate as we make a renewed commitment to serve it at our special (Pentecost) service next weekend.

Intimacy without involvement is self-absorbed. Involvement without intimacy is spiritually bankrupt. Only the rich blend of intimacy with God and involvement with others echoes the spirituality of Jesus – only this is a faith that works!

1 FAMILY

"SO THEY SAY ..."

*No one was ever heard to say
on their deathbed,
'I wish I had spent more
time at the office.'* [6]

"SO THEY SAY ..."

*A father to the fatherless,
a defender of widows,
is God in his holy dwelling.
God sets the lonely in families ...*

Psalm 68:5-6

START HERE

Families matter. Like small bricks in a larger wall, the strength of each family in your area can have a massive impact on the local community as a whole. Remove a few bricks, and the wall stands. Remove a few more bricks, though, and the very infrastructure of the community begins to crumble or even to crash. God is passionate about mums, dads, aunts, cousins, kids, godfathers, grandparents and babies, simply because he loves people and is committed to human relationships! Our own experience of family life may be tinged with disappointment, but God has a positive dream for families and communities that he is longing to outwork, even in the most difficult situations.

We glimpse God's embracing passion for families several times in the Old Testament. The Psalms relate how God responds to those suffering loneliness by placing them in families (Ps. 68:5-6); the Psalms also celebrate the positive vibrancy of cities and communities where children are received as a gift from his hand (Ps. 127:3-5). The New Testament, in turn, uses the concept of family or household more than any other to describe the church – this outwardly embracing community of heavenly-minded people on planet earth.

If your 24-7 Prayer week is going to focus on the family (or relationships/friendships more generally) then this part of the *Prayerworks* manual is for you. It's full of ideas for you and your church or group to pray and act so that you can empower, protect and celebrate family life.

It's important to be aware from the start that family issues are sometimes the hardest ones to pray about and to deal with. They are, literally, close to home and can be very painful for people. That's not a reason for *avoiding* this theme, but an encouragement to approach it with wisdom, sensitivity and forward-thinking. Plan clearly and carefully about how you would like to pray about the family, and, if necessary, have people available who are trained in dealing with family or relationship matters at certain points during your week of around-the-clock prayer.

THE BIBLE ON ... FAMILY

Based on: Genesis chapters 1-4, 6-9, 27; the book of Ruth, 1 Samuel 1-2,

Our families are shrinking. UK trends indicate that, while there were 5.8 million households containing only one person in 1996, in 2011 there will be around 7.9 million such households. That's an increase of over a third in just fifteen years – which is all the more striking when you consider that 88% per cent of us say we consider family to be the single most important thing in our lives.[7]

However, not only are our families shrinking – our concept of family itself has also shrunk. The western notion that family equals two parents plus two point four children was always foreign to the cultures of the Bible and the overwhelming majority of other cultures too. It is we, the West, who are the odd ones out; 'family', for most human beings, means the whole social network of blood relatives, in multiple branches and generations, and often many friends in the wider community too.

The Bible, then, is not unique in exploding our idea of family – most cultures do that for us. Yet it is unique in another way: the Bible claims God invented family, saw it fall apart, then came to the rescue.

The condensed version of the story goes something like this: human beings, male and female, were created by God and commanded to care for and fill the earth. However, the delight of both sexual union and the ensuing family growth through new offspring were soon marred by devastating violence (e.g. Cain and Abel) and sibling rivalry (e.g. Jacob and Esau), all of which Genesis records with startling honesty. However, within the Old Testament fabric of fallen human history are woven some golden threads. The stories of Noah and his family; Ruth, Naomi and Boaz; Hannah and Samuel; all these point the way to a brighter future and a God who redeems and restores broken families. The Lord's strong commitment to community relationships is further underlined by the 'children of Israel' concept – the portrait of an entire nation as one family – which is reflected in Israel's repeated use of genealogies.

Jesus, as usual, takes things even further and deeper. Through him we discover that spiritual family is as real as physical family. 'Who are my mother and my brothers?' he asks. 'Those who hear my words and obey them!' It's clear that Jesus' most important relationship is with his heavenly Father, and he intends his followers to have the same Father-child relationship – even to the exclusion of their own fathers, mothers and siblings, if need be, in the pursuit of God's kingdom. The earthly implications of Jesus' life and message, however, are not anti-family but strongly pro-family. In Jesus, the idea of family is even more extended – both upward and outward. The New Testament records that now, everyone can be part of God's family – not just Abraham's children. We are chosen and adopted as children of

God. That heavenly security enables us to become agents of earthly change. Suddenly, the spiritual gets practical again! That's why time and again Paul's letters instruct householders (parents/children, husbands/wives, masters/servants) to honour Christ by honouring each other.

Exploring the concept of family in the Bible means being prepared to explode, extend and re-learn what families, childlikeness, fatherhood, adoption and relationship are really all about. In a messed-up world where loneliness is normal and families falter and fail, how desperately we need God to expand our shrunken view and heal our relationships, re-creating 'family' exactly the way he first intended it to be.

See also Romans 8:15-17, Galatians 3:7 and James 1:27.

GEARING UP

Key questions to ask yourself/your church:

- Think about your church community and what you know of the family experiences of those in your church.
- As a church *community*, what ways have you found actively to support one another and to work out your faith in your family lives?
- What more could you do as a church?
- What ways are you currently engaging, *as a church community*, in the family lives of people in your surrounding community, particularly those who find family life difficult or painful, for whatever reason?
- What more could you do within the surrounding community?

Key community sectors to consider engaging with:

- The Samaritans
- Counselling agencies
- Help the Aged
- Relate (relationship and marriage counselling)
- Residents and staff of local residential/care homes
- Mother and toddler groups

INTIMACY AND INVOLVEMENT

Real-life Stories of Faith in Action

DEBT CRISIS FAMILY GIVES HOLIDAYS TO FRIENDS

Hello, my name is Diane Briggs. For the last thirteen years, I have worked as a manager in a church-based pre-school in a deprived area of our town.

One of the main aims of the church is to serve our local community, and over the years I have made friends with many families here. I believe that as a Christian, wherever I go and whatever I do, I take Jesus with me. The pre-school has a support network of people who pray for us regularly and the Christian staff always pray together, each morning and afternoon, before the children arrive. Staff who are not Christians sometimes ask for prayers for their friends and family too!

I remember a mum from our mother and toddler group who had just had Shawn, her second child. Shawn had a serious feeding problem and instead of thriving, he looked like a very malnourished baby. I asked the mother if I could pray for him, to which she readily agreed. So, for three months, every time she came into the building someone prayed for that child. Gradually, his feeding started to improve and today he is a healthy little boy attending primary school.

Another mother, Lisa, once told me that her family were about to lose their home. They had fallen behind with their mortgage and could not find a way of catching up with the repayments. This was putting relationships in the family under a lot of strain. I asked if she would mind if I said a prayer with her. Lisa was desperate and she quickly said 'yes'.

I prayed a simple prayer asking God to help them see a way forward.

Yet to my surprise, I also found myself asking God to provide them with a holiday, to give them an opportunity to spend time together as a family. Under the circumstances I knew this was impossible; there was simply no money for holidays. However, the next time I saw Lisa she was thrilled to tell me that a friend of theirs had asked her husband to do some decorating for them. The payment? One week in a caravan at the seaside! Some years later, they now have their own caravan and are even offering holidays to their friends who don't get a break!

Of course, I don't always pray <u>with</u> the families I work with. Often I just pray <u>for</u> them, mostly without them even knowing. But God constantly reminds me of a saying my mother frequently used in our family, " If you don't ask, you don't get!"

CREATIVE PRAYER

PARTY TIME

Throw a surprise party for an individual or a group of people in your local community, then offer to pray with them, as part of your prayer week. Jesus seemed to spend much of his time at dinner parties – it's a great example to follow and (believe it or not) such a celebratory atmosphere should in fact be a very natural place for us to pray.

FAMILY FACTS AND FIGURES

Get hold of some statistics relating to family to fuel your prayers. One good source is the National Statistics website: www.statistics.gov.uk. Alternatively, national organisations such as Childline or Relate, or newspaper articles often have plenty of facts and figures about family life. There are any number of ways you can use information like this to fuel prayer – just be careful not to overload people with data or they'll feel a bit swamped. You could place different family facts around your prayer room, or email one key statistic with a relevant Bible verse each day to those who have signed up on the rota, or print them in your weekly news sheet in the run up to your week.

A PRAYER FOR PRODIGALS

Lord, hear our prayer for our prodigals:

We pray for parents, friends and family of prodigals to be released from false guilt
Help us to be more vulnerable with each other
Help us to stop judging each other, especially where it involves our children
Help us to forgive those who, through harsh words or actions, may have played a part in the creation of our prodigals
Help us to create local churches that care about the things that really matter to you and that are full of love and acceptance
We lift our prodigals to you by name. You know where they are, what they are doing, and their very hearts. Touch them now, we pray.
Grant that we may be delivered from the spirit of the elder brother

So Lord, we bring to the foot of the cross those we love.
In your mercy, bring them home.
Amen

Adapted from: *Care for the Family bookmarks*. www.prodigals.org.uk

POP, FILM AND TV 'TRIGGERS'

that you could use in a prayer event on the theme of family:

Family Portrait by Pink

We Are Family by Sister Sledge

1980 by Estelle

The Simpsons

Eastenders

About A Boy

The Waltons

American Beauty

Meet The Parents

Billy Elliot

Love Actually

Brady Bunch

Stepmom

My Family

Mrs Doubtfire

DRESSING UP GAMES

Kids love dressing up. Set any kids you are responsible for a challenge: to dress like the prodigal son at all four stages of the story – at home (casual dress), at parties (not too wild, perhaps ...?!), on the farm (feeding pigs) and at the celebration feast (robe, ring, sandals and so on). It could be a great way of teaching the biblical story within individual families, in kids' clubs or as a Sunday school activity – and a fun prelude to prayer based on the same story. Take photos of them at different stages of the story, and stick those photos up in your prayer room. Encourage the children you are responsible for to draw, paint or write their prayers or feelings as a result of this game, and display those creative prayers in your prayer room alongside the photos. This activity will, of course, require some preparation in terms of costumes, cameras and creative materials for the pray-ers themselves.

THE FAMILY OF GOD: A MEDITATION AND PRAYER

'In the last days, God says,
I will pour out my Spirit on all people.
Your sons and daughters will prophesy,
your young men will see visions,
your old men will dream dreams.
Even on my servants, both men and women,
I will pour out my Spirit in those days,
and they will prophesy'

Acts 2: 17-18, NIV

Dreams, visions and prophecy – these are all exciting things. But did you notice the way that God's Spirit affirms relationships? Sons and daughters prophesy. Young men and old men pursue visions and dreams, complementary glimpses of the future, together. Ordinary women and men get drenched in this spiritual waterfall, together. Implicit in this startling poem is a portrait not just of how the Holy Spirit speaks and acts, but also of how the different generations and genders will flow together within the family of God. In fact, that's a great definition of what the Pentecost church should be; God's family.

Lord, renew all our relationships in the power of your Holy Spirit. Forge new and strong links between men and women, young and old, rich and poor; between different races, backgrounds and creeds. May the world say again 'See how these Christians love each other!' May your church become once more a refuge for the widow, the orphan and the refugee; for those who have lost their families; for those who are looking for a different kind of family. Reach out through us, and rescue many, as you create this new community, the family of God. Amen.

CHOCOLATE SURPRISE MEDITATION

Like the other 'sensory' meditations in Part 2 of *Prayerworks*, the chocolate surprise idea is flexible and could be used at any point during your 24-7 Prayer week. We're placed it early on in this section because it's a great way of introducing people to the idea that God can speak to us through *all* of our senses.

Preparation

- Buy large bars of chocolate, break into squares and put on plates.
- Have some quiet music ready to play while people are meditating.

Activity

Start by explaining that we are all part of the family of God, and that as our Father, our heavenly parent, he just loves giving great presents to his children. Mention too that God can speak through any part of creation. Then announce to your group that you are all going to meditate on chocolate together! Pass the plates round and ask people to take one piece of chocolate each. Once everyone has a square of chocolate, say that you are going to let them meditate for approximately five minutes before asking some volunteers to come and share what they received from God through their piece of chocolate. Encourage them to use all their senses in this meditation. Ask them to *look* at the chocolate, to *touch* it, to *smell* it and eventually to *taste* it, and to *listen* to God to see what he has to say through it – both for themselves and 'the rest of the family'. Encourage them to write down what God says. Play some instrumental music quietly during the time of meditation. After five minutes ask the group whether they have finished. If so, ask for two or three volunteers to tell the others in the group what they received from God. You will be amazed at what people get through a piece of chocolate! This exercise not only encourages people to use their senses to hear from God, but it also gives opportunities for them to participate. This builds both their confidence and their sense of identity as valued members of God's family.

Adapted from: *50 Creative Worship Ideas – For the Whole Church and Small Groups* by Nancy Goudie, p34-35. www.nancygoudie.com

GO AND DO THIS ... ACTIVE PRAYER

STEP 1: Get a map of your area and pinpoint the top five locations where families gather with pins or dot stickers – that could be the shops, cinema, playground, parks or somewhere else entirely!

STEP 2: Organise a family ramble (that's family in its broadest sense – everyone's invited) that joins the points or dots on the map. Visit every location once and pray at that location.

STEP 3: Feedback to each other afterwards (a hot cuppa and a custard cream biscuit may help) about what needs struck you the most, what God was saying, and what you might do next.

PRAYER POINTERS

- Pray for a new compassion for the young – the unborn child, babies and toddlers.

- Pray that the engulfing tide of family breakdown is turned back.

- Pray for strong parenting role models to emerge in your community – especially for those parents from broken family backgrounds.

- Pray for the 'reconstituted' or 'blended' families near you – where divorce or bereavement has meant that one or more parents have remarried and brought children with them from a previous relationship.

- Pray for parents who are growing older and more frail, making the hard transition from being parents to being 'the parented'.

GET CONNECTED - FAMILY

Some Christian agencies that can support and inform you

Care for the Family aims to promote strong family life and to help those hurting because of family breakdown.

Tel: 029 2081 1733   Email: mail@cff.org.uk
Website: www.care-for-the-family.org.uk

Caritas – Social Action seeks to promote Catholic social action within the church and in society as a whole.

Tel: 020 7901 4875   Email: caritas@cbcew.org.uk
Website: www.caritas-socialaction.org.uk

For books on the subject of the family, see the book lists in the Resources section at the back of the book.

---

[6] Rob Parsons, *The Sixty Second Father,* (London: Hodder and Stoughton, 1997)

[7] The Women's National Commission, *Future Female – A 21st Century Gender Perspective,* (London: Crown Copyright 2000) pp 10-11

2 EDUCATION

> ## "SO THEY SAY ..."
>
> *Education is not the filling of a pail, but the lighting of a fire.*
>
> W.B. Yeats

> ## "SO THEY SAY ..."
>
> *The vision is an army of young people. You see bones? I see an army. And they are free from materialism ...*
>
> *The Vision*, Pete Greig

START HERE

Education is always a political hot potato. And rightly so: how and what we teach our children says a lot about our culture and makes a massive difference to society as a whole, ten or twenty years down the road.

In the UK, a sizeable proportion of our educational institutions, including many universities and schools, were started by Christian communities. Faith-based education is nothing new. You could say that since everyone believes *something*, there is no such thing as education that's not faith-based. The real debate, however, is not about whether or not schools should be faith-based – it's about deciding what principles we want to pass on. Education is more about our ethos and our values than it is about knowledge and information.

If you have the desire to make a practical and prayerful difference in the sphere of education, that's a great start in itself. God is an educator, a trainer and a coach. As you pray and get involved in the educational sphere, you'll be tapping into one of the strongest desires of the Holy Spirit, which is to teach (Jn. 14:26).

Spend serious hours during your prayer week engaging with the Teacher of teachers, sitting at the feet of the Master, asking questions and pouring out your concern for the schools and youth of your community. Encourage others with a similar passion to do the same. Then start asking 'What should we do next?' Get serious about becoming a governor, pass on your vocational skills, or even … consider starting a school where you are.

Does that sound crazy? We think so! But whether your first step is a whispered prayer or a wide-eyed dream, don't be afraid to set out on a journey of lifelong learning, education and discovery that will eventually bring great benefit to your local community. And may God give you all the wisdom you need to fulfil the task.

THE BIBLE ON ... EDUCATION

Deuteronomy 4, Proverbs, Colossians

Does God care about education? He certainly cares about what children are taught. He insisted that Israel should pass on to their children and children's children all that he had commanded them and everything they had seen him do for them during the Exodus. The first history lessons were to be about God and his dealings with his people. Those lessons would show his character, his concern, who he was and how he acted. And why is that information important? Because God knew that 'the fear of the Lord is the beginning of wisdom' (Prov. 1:7). What we think about God's character, expressed in the world he has created – we might call it our 'worldview' – will affect everything else about us. The book of Proverbs stresses again and again that we need sound instruction, leading to right thinking, in order to lead godly lives.

God's concern with Israel's schooling wasn't just that individuals should live properly. He wanted the whole nation to be an object lesson to the countries around of what could be achieved by a people living in right relationship with him. This is still his aim. Solomon's kingdom in particular attracted a lot of attention from the nations round about, as a country who were 'getting it right' generally, and whose people were enjoying the benefits. Solomon didn't restrict himself to theology or government, either – he was also a lecturer in biology and botany (1 Kgs. 4:29-34). All truth is God's truth – God made us with minds that can explore and understand the universe.

Jesus, of course, claimed he was the Truth. And in the great commission (Mt. 28:19), Jesus, the very source of truth itself, tells his followers to 'go and make disciples, teaching them...' Education – the lifelong pursuit of learning, wisdom, knowledge and understanding – is one of the foundations of our life in Christ. Romans 12:1-4 teaches us that the renewal of the mind is the pathway to transformation. Colossians is full of encouragement to know and live by the truth, to take seriously the need to 'have the full riches of complete understanding' (Col. 2:2-4). See also Colossians 1:6,7; 9,10; 2:8; 3:1-4,16-17. Scratch beneath the surface, and the Bible has much to reveal about God's care and concern for education.

GEARING UP

Key questions to ask yourself/your church:

- Create a list of all the individual people within your church community who work, volunteer or participate in (as pupils/students) the field of education.

- As a church community, what ways have you found actively to support these people and help them to work out their faith in this context?

- What more could you do as a church?

- What ways are you currently engaging, *as a church community*, in education in your surrounding community?

- What more could you do in the surrounding community? What ways can you serve, encourage and support local nurseries, schools, colleges and alternative education projects, etc.?

Key community sectors to consider engaging with:

- Nurseries

- Schools

- Colleges

- Universities

- Libraries

- Local Education Authority (LEA)

- Adult education centres

Real-life Stories of Faith in Action

BEING A PASTOR, TEACHER AND PRAYER ACTIVIST

My name is Catriona Martin. I taught at a secondary school for ten years, and now train those wanting to deliver Personal Social and Health Education in schools, as part of Oasis Esteem.

I found that in my teaching, prayer made a real difference. It helped me to have the grace, strength and wisdom to deal with the challenges that many teachers face daily, such as disruptive students.

One important aspect of teaching that may not be so obvious is having pastoral responsibility for students, which involves helping young people with their issues and needs. This might be dealing with a personal issue, such as low self-esteem, difficulties with friends, problems with studying, or family concerns, such as bereavement and separation.

Schools are 'communities within communities', so this aspect is not just confined to students but also includes supporting parents, and colleagues within the school, with issues that life generates. Being able to listen, to offer help where possible and to pray for these situations is sometimes a challenge but is also a real privilege.

CREATIVE PRAYER

GO AND DO THIS ... ACTIVE PRAYER

Offer local schools the opportunity of a prayer box for a week, where pupils can place anonymous prayer requests. Explain to the headteacher that someone will visit the school each day to take away the requests and that they will be prayed for specifically later on that same day. This way you make repeated contact rather than just an one-off contact. Make it as easy as possible for children to use the box – instructions, paper and pens are all a good idea. Perhaps there will be an opportunity for you to do an assembly or lesson and explain the Christian tradition of prayer with reference to a Bible story. You could even invite staff, pupils and their parents to visit your prayer room – it's amazing what an impact the creativity can have on people who would never otherwise dream of going into a church building.

POP, FILM AND TV 'TRIGGERS'
that you could use in a prayer event on the theme of education:

Another Brick in the Wall (Part 2) by Pink Floyd

What I go to school for by Busted

Baggy Trousers by Madness

Dead Poets' Society

Mona Lisa Smile

Pay It Forward

Mean Girls

Good Will Hunting

Dawson's Creek

Byker Grove

Hollyoaks

Grange Hill

School of Rock

MULTIPLYING OUR GIFTS – A GROUP ACTIVITY

This activity would work best for a group of between ten and twenty people, and would probably take thirty to forty-five minutes to complete well, especially if you do the feedback at the end of it.

STEP 1: Ask everyone to pray silently and ask God to show them one gift that he has given to them. Play some background music, if you like, while people are waiting on God. The 'gifts' could be a natural talent such as public speaking, or a learned gift such as playing a music instrument. Alternatively, it might be a gift of the Spirit such as prophecy, or a fruit of the Spirit such as patience. It might even be a character trait such as the ability to pioneer new things, or simple 'stickability' in the face of a crisis.

STEP 2: Once a few minutes have passed, instruct the group to start asking God who else in the room they can give their gift to. Explain that in giving our gifts away, we don't lose them, we simply multiply them into someone else's life. Read Acts 20:35, where Jesus is quoted as saying that 'It is more blessed to give than to receive.'

STEP 3: Invite people, when they feel ready, to go over to each person that they believe God has spoken to them about, lay one hand on their shoulder, and pray for them to receive the same gift they already have themselves. Allow people the freedom to do this silently, but encourage verbal prayers, even if short or quiet, as a way of bringing outward expression to what God is speaking internally to people's hearts.

Ask for feedback immediately after this exercise, using some of the following questions. This might well be the best bit – it's a great way to encourage and affirm one another.

- What gift(s) do you think God has given to you?
- What did you feel or sense as someone else was praying for you?
- Did God say or show you anything unusual?
- What obvious gifts do we see in others around us in this room that they have not identified for themselves?
- How can we all give gifts from God to other people in our everyday lives?

PUTTING ON YOUR L-PLATES...

Get hold of a pair of L-plates as a reminder that you are a disciple on a spiritual journey, and always a learner. Place them in your prayer room as an aid to visual meditation on discipleship.

Prayerworks: Part 2

72

You might want to meditate on the verse 'Lord, teach us to pray' (Lk. 11:1). While doing so, thank God quite simply that this means you are free from having to be perfect at anything, that his grace is sufficient for every need that arises, and that there is always more to discover in God. Next, ask him to enable you to be a good role model and teacher of others – yet one who is always willing to learn new and deeper lessons from the source of all Wisdom.

Before you leave the prayer room, write out a short explanation for those who come after you that describes how people are to hold or look at the L-plate(s) while asking God to teach them what it means to be a disciple, learner and follower of Jesus.

'WHOLE PERSON' EDUCATION –
A TRUE STORY TO INSPIRE PRAYER

Education is the most powerful weapon which you can use to change the world.
NELSON MANDELA

The important thing is not to stop questioning.
ALBERT EINSTEIN

Oasis Academy Enfield, a City Academy for 11-18 year olds, opens in North London in 2007. The Academy will provide a rich and balanced educational environment which caters for the whole person – academically, vocationally, socially, morally, spiritually, emotionally and environmentally. Its task is to serve students as well as to provide a learning hub for the entire community. In this way it will raise aspirations, unlock potential and work to achieve excellence through encouraging a 'can do' culture which nurtures confident and competent people. By raising the aspirations of young people and ensuring that they have access to high-quality education, regardless of their faith or ability, Oasis aims to ensure that its ethos of innovation and inclusiveness are put to use in developing a City Academy for the whole local community.

Prayer-and-action points

- Reflect on the quotes from Nelson Mandela and Albert Einstein, and their impact in the fields of race relations and science respectively. Pray for a similar hunger for wisdom, learning and education to be born in the life of someone you know who is not yet part of a church community.

- Using a map, locate all your local schools, colleges or other educational institutions. Pray for 'whole person education' to become a living reality in your community, and especially for Christian educators who play a key part in realising that ambition.

PRAYER POINTERS ON EDUCATION

- Find the names of your local headteachers, phoning schools if necessary to do so. Find out the most pressing needs each school is facing and commit to praying for them daily during your prayer week.

- Thank God for the positive heritage of faith-based schools in the UK and the positive attitude of Government towards all faith communities.

- Actively bless someone from a faith community different to your own. Why not visit them and look for ways of expressing unconditional love?

- Spend a day of your prayer week listening to God for ways that you can disciple, mentor, coach or teach people of all ages in your local area.

- Become a school governor or board member and get an inside perspective that will fuel your intercession, as well as challenge, stretch and grow your faith. (Contact CARE for Education, as below, for more information on how to do this.)

EXPLORING GOD'S SPIRIT AS 'TEACHER'

In different places in the Bible, the Holy Spirit is described as the Spirit of truth, wisdom, knowledge and understanding. That's pretty educational stuff! Some people say that Jesus was a great teacher – perhaps that's because he oozed the wisdom of God through his Spirit. How do you think the Holy Spirit helps each of us in the process of life-long learning? What difference can he make in our schools? How is he active in the way parents educate their children during out-of-school hours? Does the Spirit only work in faith-based schools or in all schools? What difference does it make to my life to see Jesus as my mentor, tutor or life-coach?

EDUCATIONAL PRAYER TOUR

Take a small group of people on a prayer tour of schools in your area. You should do this discreetly and with sensitivity, preferably during out-of-school hours (unless you happen to be a parent!). Stand outside the gates of each school and listen out for specific prayer themes or practical instructions which you sense God is speaking to you. You could even lay hands on the walls of the schools as a symbolic act of prayer. Intercede for the hearts, minds and imaginations of children in each school, for their parents, and for teachers and other school staff.

GET CONNECTED - EDUCATION

Some Christian agencies that can support and inform you

ACT (Association of Christian Teachers) is a non-denominational membership organisation which aims to provide professional and spiritual support to all Christians engaged in pre-school, primary, special, secondary and college education in England.
Tel: 01727 840298   Email: act@christian-teachers.org.uk
Website: www.christian-teachers.org.uk

CARE is a Christian charity involved in caring, campaigning and communicating across the UK, seeking to combine practical caring initiatives with public policy on social and ethical issues. One aspect of its work deals particularly with resourcing and supporting all those involved in the field of education.
Tel: 020 7233 0455   Email: communications@care.org.uk
Website: www.care.org.uk

CARE for Education: Governor Helpline - free advice on issues relating to school governance (England and Wales) and school board members (Scotland) from a Christian perspective.
Tel: 023 9261 0689   Email: governors@care.org.uk
Website: www.care.org.uk/education

Fusion is a group of people who are working together to help catalyse and resource a radical movement for Christ among students and within their culture.
Tel: 01243 531898   Email: admin@fusion.uk.com
Website: www.fusion.uk.com

Moorlands College provides a challenging learning environment where men and women, passionate about Jesus Christ, may be nurtured and equipped to impact both church and world.
Tel: 01425 672369   Email: mailbox@moorlands.ac.uk
Website: www.moorlands.ac.uk

OAS!S Trust is committed to demonstrating the Christian faith in action. One aspect of its work is Oasis Youth Inclusion, which works actively with and on behalf of socially excluded young people.
Tel: 020 7450 9000   Email: enquiries@oasistrust.org
Website: www.oasistrust.org / www.oasistrust.org/youthinclusion

UCCF Christian Unions in the Universities and Colleges Christian Fellowship are committed together to making disciples of Jesus Christ in the student world.
Tel: 0116 255 1700 Email: email@uccf.org.uk
Website: www.uccf.org.uk

3 HEALTH, LEISURE AND WELL-BEING

"SO THEY SAY ..."

'I have come that they may have life, and have it to the full.

Jesus (John 10:10)

"SO THEY SAY ..."

It has been said that every great leader or teacher has one core message that permeates everything they do and say... It was true of Karl Marx, of Gandhi, of Martin Luther King Jr, of Freud. And it's equally true of Jesus... the core of Jesus' life-transforming, though often deeply misunderstood, message is this: **The Kingdom, the in-breaking shalom of God, is available now to everyone through me.**[8]

Steve Chalke

START HERE

Would Jesus have gone to his local gym? What's a Christian response to lengthening hospital waiting lists? Or to the HIV pandemic? Are alternative therapies all wrong? Why did the apostle Paul model his life on athletes from the sporting arena? What is there to affirm in women's magazines that talk about well-being? How should I spend my retirement years? And, above all, why all these random questions?!

In fact, there *is* a connection between all these questions (and many more like them), and it's something called 'shalom'.

'Shalom' may sound like mumbo jumbo to you and I, but it's a key biblical concept and one that's bursting with life and hope today. It embraces our modern concepts of health, leisure and well-being, but also goes much further than that. Shalom is like a tree: one strong central idea with lots of different branches. Though it's often translated as 'peace', the Hebrew word actually means something much fuller, richer, deeper: well-being or prosperity in the whole of life. Shalom is God's best for his world at every level: emotional, physical, social, financial, ecological, mental and spiritual. It's to do with all those questions above and much, much more.

Jesus, of course, is the Prince of Peace (shalom). The type of involvement we are hoping, praying and working for in our communities is nothing less than one which brings his kingdom, his well-being, to every aspect of life in our towns and cities.

If you choose just one theme for prayer and action during your Faithworks/24-7 week, you might well want to choose this one. It touches on and embraces all the others – family life; education; business and employment; politics, law and order, and the excluded. In every aspect of life, the Lord God really does want his sin-sick world to 'get well soon.' He doesn't want to throw the world in the litter-bin of history, he wants to see it rescued and saved completely.

So, encourage your church to pray and work for shalom in the streets where you live.

THE BIBLE ON ... HEALTH, LEISURE AND WELL-BEING

Based on Luke 4:14-30

> *The Spirit of the Lord is on me,*
> *because he has anointed me*
> *to preach good news to the poor.*
> *He has sent me to proclaim freedom for the prisoners*
> *and recovery of sight for the blind,*
> *to release the oppressed,*
> *to proclaim the year of the Lord's favour.*

Some people call it the 'Nazareth manifesto'. It was the day Jesus launched his public career. The day he got thrown out of the synagogue by his own townsfolk. The day he almost got thrown off a cliff. This was the day Jesus declared that because God's Spirit was resting on him, he was able to rescue the lowest of the low and truly demonstrate the good news of God's kingdom.

As political manifestos go, it hardly received a rapturous reception. As sermons go, it was too short and removed any credibility he already had, with immediate effect. But as kingdoms go, it initiated the most remarkable and most talked about revolution in human history.

It's just that this revolution is one that's all about peace not violence, and well-being (shalom), not power or control. And it's a revolution that's for everyone.

GEARING UP

Key questions to ask yourself/your church:

- Create a list of all the people within your church community who work or volunteer in the health and leisure services.

- As a church community, what ways have you found actively to support these people and help them to work out their faith in this context?

- What more could you do as a church?

- What ways are you currently engaging, *as a church community*, in the health and leisure services in your surrounding community?

- What more could you do for the surrounding community? What ways can you serve, encourage and support local hospitals and doctors' surgeries, clinics and health centres ... and maybe even gyms and spas (etc.)?

Key community sectors to consider engaging with:

- Doctors and health professionals

- Fitness and leisure operators

- Alternative therapists

- Your local library

- Recreational facility managers

Real-life Stories of Faith in Action

HEAVEN IS A PARTY

Sarah Smith is helping to pioneer the 24-7 Prayer clubbing project.

'Are you are on pills?' That was the question I was asked by a guy standing near me as I was bopping away to the sounds of DJ Steve Lawler at a club called The End. 'No', I replied. 'Really?' he said, looking puzzled. 'You look like you are!'

I explained that I was just very into the music and didn't need pills to enhance my club experience. I then went on to say that I was with a group of friends and none of us were on pills. He couldn't believe it. All of his mates had been pill popping and were in the other room crashed out and in no state to join him on the dance floor. Then I told him that we were all Christians and were spending our time communicating with God as we danced. He nearly dropped his bottle of beer in surprise! He thought it was great though and made the interesting comment that he liked being around 'clean' people.

A group of us had gone out clubbing and praying together, as a new and growing 24-7 Prayer and Mission Team, as part of a 'club and pray tour' around seven of the most influential clubs in London. We are a group of people who are passionate about God and passionate about clubbing and God has been showing us that he is overwhelmingly passionate about the clubbing community. In fact, he is desperate to bring transformation to the lives of clubbers in London, the UK and all over the world.

So far, our club and pray tour has taken us to Turnmills, the Ministry of Sound and The End, praying as the Spirit leads us, worshipping and being completely open to what he wants us to do. We are also planning to go to Heaven very soon!

Yet this all feels like just the first stage of something bigger that is still to come. We'd love to be able to start building relationships with people and to 'be Jesus' to them where we can. We are not sure how this will happen or what it will look like, but God does – he has the plan!

God has already been moving in Ibiza and Ayia Napa where 24-7 Mission Teams have been serving him throughout the summer for the past few years. Back in the UK, Christian clubbers, DJs, dancers, promoters and music makers are being raised up to do God-stuff. A group of us from all over the place (Portsmouth, Southampton, Bournemouth, Reading, Guildford, Woking, Bognor Regis, London, Sheffield and Bristol) met up recently in Southampton to share and pray together. We're all involved in different areas: holding club nights, discipling clubbing mates, clubbing and praying etc. But we are one big team making ourselves available to God to do his thing in clubland and looking forward to what he has in store.

CREATIVE PRAYER

VIDEO DIARIES

Visit several local hotspots where shalom is definitely absent, with a video camera. Film what you see – no more and no less – and play it on a TV inside your prayer room with a sign next to it simply saying, 'Please pray for the well-being of our community.'

THE JESUS MANIFESTO

Get hold of one or more manifestos from mainstream political parties. Compare and contrast them with Jesus' own manifesto from Luke chapter 4 (see the beginning of this chapter). Then pray. Why not write a letter to your local MP explaining that you have been praying for their success in promoting the well-being of the constituency?

A variation on this would be to consider how different our westernised version of well-being is to the biblical concept of well-being, with the help of magazines and newspaper articles, alongside Bible stories that talk about peace/shalom/well-being. A collage created out of this could be a powerful visual addition to your prayer room.

POP, FILM AND TV 'TRIGGERS'
that you could use in a prayer event on the theme of health, leisure and well-being:

Sunny Afternoon by The Kinks

Easy Like Sunday Morning by Lionel Richie

Long Hot Summer by The Style Council

Supersize Me

Fight Club

Patch Adams

ER

Casualty

The Brittas Empire

'TACTILE REFLECTION STATION' ACTIVITY

Aim

To challenge participants to think about their own health but not just in terms of physical health, and to also be challenged about who is or is not healthy in their community.

Materials required

- Objects connected with health/unhealthiness
- OHP, transparencies and images
- Bibles
- Pens and paper

Activity

Create a 'tactile reflection station'. Collect lots of objects and symbols of health. These can be empty medicine bottles, doctors' equipment, fruit, vitamins etc. Also collect objects of unhealthy things like junk food, drugs, dirty things etc. – though make sure everything you use is safe! Alternatively or in addition, set up an OHP and project (on the wall/floor/ceiling/old bed sheet from behind) some images of health/unhealthiness. You can gather some from magazines and photocopy them on to transparencies. Such images could include: friendships, hamburgers, diseased people in the developing world, hospitals etc.

People are to use this as a place to pray/reflect/sit/think about the idea of their own health and that of their communities. In this reflective environment, give each participant one of the following sets of instructions on an explanation card.

Explanation card 1

Reflect and meditate on these objects and the images of health. Pick them up, touch them and ask God to speak to you. What do you think of as healthy? Are you healthy? Who and where are the unhealthy in your community?

- Read: Proverbs 13:12 and Proverbs 17:22.
- Meditate on these passages about health and ask God to speak to you.

Explanation card 2

While holding one of these objects or looking at one of these images, pray:

- For your own health, that out of strength God will enable you to bless others.
- For the health of your community, that God will heal the sick and strengthen those who care for them.
- For the health of the world: that those with health and wealth on their side will 'spend themselves' on behalf of those who have neither.

Read through Isaiah 58 as you reflect on issues of health and wholeness.[9]

3 HEALTH, LEISURE AND WELL-BEING

GOD'S HARMONY IN THE WHOLE OF LIFE – A REFLECTION ON SHALOM

God's purpose for us as we pray and enjoy a deep relationship with him is that we should experience his peace. The Hebrew word 'shalom' can best be translated with our word 'harmony', a deeply peaceful relationship.[10]

Harmony with God

We enter into a deeply harmonious relationship with God the Father, through faith in Christ. We have all seen older married couples who just seem so deeply 'at one' together, enjoying a genuinely harmonious love. Our life with God is meant to be just like that (Eph. 2:14-18).

Harmony within ourselves

God's shalom also produces a deep peace inside of us, the ability to live at peace with ourselves. In this era of insecurity and depression we can only stand amazed at God's loving grace which brings us such an inner shalom (Jn. 14:27).

Harmony with God's people

The New Testament commands us to live in shalom with our Christian brothers and sisters. Among the people of God, loving peace and harmony are to reign (Col. 3:15).

Harmony with all people

But this is not a ghetto-existence. It is a calling to reach out in love and peace to everyone. We are commanded, as far as we are able, to live at peace with all people (Rom. 12:18).

Such shalom is a gift from God. It can only come from God, for it is beyond our human ability.

SHALOM PRAYER POINTERS

- Pray for the promotion of healthy lifestyles – diet, exercise, rest, relationships – in your locality.
- Target one of the elements above (e.g. diet) and improve that element of your lifestyle for a week or a month to start with.
- Fast from something like TV, food, sleep, eating out or films, either alone or with other pray-ers, for a short while.
- Dedicate any money or time saved by your fast to God.
- Pray that God would show you creative ways of supporting those who work in the fields of health and/or leisure.

WOODWORKING SKILLS AND ADDICTION COUNSELLING IN THE SHETLAND ISLES

– a true story to inspire prayer

In the remote setting of the Shetland Isles, a region with some of the highest alcohol abuse rates in the UK, the Turning Point Craft Initiative is a popular therapy programme amongst recovering drug and alcohol addicts. By combining woodworking and wood-turning skills with addiction counselling, the project is helping a number of local people come to terms with their addiction. The initiative has been pioneered by Kenny Williamson, a life-long Shetland resident and committed Christian who himself struggled with alcohol addiction earlier in life. The idea of combining his woodworking skills with his addiction counselling experience came from his wife, Pat. Although she died of cancer in 2002, Kenny has been able to deal with the pain of her death, finding purpose in helping drug and alcohol addicts through the recovery process.[11]

- Thank God for positive projects and stories like the one above, which bring practical well-being, healing and hope to many people.

- Pray for those trapped by addictions such as drugs and alcohol, and for those who work patiently and bravely to break the cycle of abuse.

- Gather a small group of people to pray into this particular issue once or twice during your prayer week.

- Ask God to show you if there is anything your church or community should do as a first step to becoming the answer to your own prayers.

GET CONNECTED – HEALTH, LEISURE AND WELL-BEING

Some Christian agencies that can support and inform you

24-7 Prayer exists to transform the world through a movement of Christ-centred and mission-minded prayer. For several years 24-7 has been sending mission teams to some of the heartlands of dance and leisure – Ibiza and Ayia Napa.
Tel: 020 7557 4620   Email: info@24-7prayer.com
Website: www.24-7prayer.com / www.24-7mission.com

CARE is a Christian charity involved in caring, campaigning and communicating across the UK. It seeks to combine practical caring initiatives with public policy on social and ethical issues.
Tel: 020 7233 0455   Email: communications@care.org.uk
Websites: www.care.org.uk   www.care.org.uk/education

Caritas – Social Action seeks to promote Catholic social action within the church and in society as a whole.
Tel: 020 7901 4875   Email: caritas@cbcew.org.uk
Website: www.caritas-socialaction.org.uk

Nancy Goudie has produced a number of books and CDs about spiritual wholeness and runs popular 'spiritual health weekends'. She directs NGM (new generation music and mission), together with her husband Ray.
Tel: 01454 414880   Email: info@ngm.org.uk
Website: www.nancygoudie.com / www.ngm.org.uk

OAS!S Trust is committed to demonstrating the Christian faith in action. It works in communities across the world, seeking to provide holistic solutions to the major social issues of our time.
Tel: 020 7450 9000   Email: enquiries@oasistrust.org
Website: www.oasistrust.org

[8] Steve Chalke and Alan Mann, *The Lost Message of Jesus,* (Grand Rapids: Zondervan, 2003)

[9] Adapted from material supplied by Blythe Toll and Gerard Kelly. Copyright 2004 The Bless Network (*www.bless.org.uk*)

[10] This material was supplied by Martin Goldsmith, All Nations Christian College

[11] The Turning Point Craft Initiative was chosen to receive the 2004 Spring Harvest Faithworks Community Innovation Award

4 BUSINESS AND EMPLOYMENT

> ## "SO THEY SAY ..."
> *We are convinced that England will never be converted until the laity use the opportunities daily afforded by their various professions, crafts and occupations.*[12]

> ## "SO THEY SAY ..."
> *Such heroes are as radical on Monday morning as Sunday night. They don't need fame from names. Instead they grin quietly upwards and hear the crowds chanting again and again: 'COME ON!'*
>
> *The Vision*, Pete Greig

START HERE

IDEAS AND RESOURCES FOR YOUR PRAYER WEEK

Let's play 'word association'. If I say 'work', what pops into your head – boredom, workaholics, characters from *The Office*, slave-driver bosses, endless paperwork or unpaid overtime, perhaps? How about fulfilment, satisfaction, gift, stewardship or creativity?

Ever since Eden, human beings have worked. Undoubtedly, work can be pretty demanding at times – which does itself create both challenges and opportunities for the church to serve its local community. However, work is in fact a good thing, and it's a God-thing. In Ephesians 2:10 we are told that we are all 'God's workmanship, created in Christ Jesus to do good works'. Notice the connection? The real work is what God is doing in us …

Every week, large numbers of us spend a couple of hours sitting in church. Yet we probably also spend thirty to forty hours working (or more if you're a full-time parent!). That's why work, business and employment are key themes for any prayer week. If we're not praying about working lives, then perhaps we should wonder what we *are* praying about?

Some of us need reminding that 'faith without works is dead.' Others of us need some persuasion to stop working for a bit and get Sabbath time – e.g. in a prayer room. All of us, however, need a little encouragement to realise that we are 'full-time ministers' in our workplaces, wherever and whatever those workplaces may be. Most of us would also agree that our own church could engage better with employers and employees in our locality.

This section is designed to inspire reflection, prayer, thought and creative action, all centred on just these sorts of work-based issues, and to heighten awareness of the needs of those in the workplace, for those groups that want to major on this topic for their own community involvement.

THE BIBLE ON ... BUSINESS AND EMPLOYMENT

Based on the book of Nehemiah

Then I prayed to the God of heaven, and I answered the king, "If it pleases the king and if your servant has found favour in his sight, let him send me to the city in Judah where my fathers are buried so that I can rebuild it"

(Nehemiah 2:4-5)

Nehemiah was both a project manager and a prayer warrior. For him, action was spiritual and prayer was practical. He had no artificial divide between what was sacred and what was secular – all of it was worship, poured out in practical, everyday, working life.

Of course, people's working lives can be hard to survive in, let alone worship in. Nehemiah and his team faced physical threats and intimidation as they sought to rebuild Jerusalem's city wall. He even had to instruct his builders to act as soldiers: shovel in one hand, sword in the other. Yet throughout their multiple difficulties, which were phenomenal, they simply *refused* to stop praying – and that's a thread which runs through the entire story. The book of Nehemiah is peppered with prayers sent up to the God of heaven.

Here is one group that knows both their own human limits and the power of their God. In the end, they triumph against the odds and rebuild a city in a matter of days. How do they do it? With an integrated spirituality that blends work and worship together, and thereby avoids any hint of an artificial divide between the two.

God is interested in both our work and our workers, as several of the Old Testament prophets make clear. It's time we prayed for professionals, for entrepreneurs, for family-run businesses, for multi-national corporations, for low-paid shop workers, and for all the rest as well.

GEARING UP

Key questions to ask yourself/your church:

- Gather a list of all the people within your church community (perhaps excluding others that are highlighted elsewhere in the week) who are employed.
- As a church community, what ways have you found actively to support these people and help them to work out their faith in this context?
- What more could you do as a church?
- What ways are you currently engaging, *as a church community*, in local businesses and employment projects in your surrounding community?
- What more could you do for your surrounding community? What ways can you serve, encourage and support local shops and businesses, employment projects and training schemes?

Key community sectors to consider engaging with:

- Your local Chamber of Commerce
- Your three biggest local employers
- Job Centre staff
- Christians running local businesses

INTIMACY AND INVOLVEMENT

Real-life Stories of Faith in Action

SHIPPING MONEY FOR GOD

My name is Andrew Southwood. I am forty years old, and married with two sons.

I trained as a banker and have been in the banking industry since the age of nineteen, specialising in financing deep sea cargo ships. For the last eleven years I have owned and run a financial consultancy in the shipping industry. We assist ship-owners with financing their ships, and banks with lending to ship-owners. In addition, I have also helped to start a number of other businesses.

God has called me to be in the workplace, so I try to do every aspect of my job as though I'm working for him. This sphere of work provides some great opportunities to meet people who would never normally come into contact with the church. Each of us in business or employment can be a positive 'kingdom' influence for such people, through both our actions and our words.

I try to run my business as if God is the Chairman, which means he is wholly involved in the decision-making. I try to run the finances of my business on the basis that God owns it all and I am simply his manager. And I try to treat the staff with the same grace with which God loves and accepts me.

I hope that each of my businesses will attract people within their spheres of influence to Jesus, will be positive places to work and will make substantial profits in order to fund the work of advancing his kingdom.

CREATIVE PRAYER

A NEHEMIAH-STYLE NIGHT HIKE

During your prayer week, take a night-time tour of your community with a few friends, just like Nehemiah did (Neh. 2:11-20). Wrap up, wear walking boots and take some hot drinks and a map with you if you're taking the concept of a night hike more literally! Even a short walk, though, can be illuminating and educational.

Often the night watches are times to hear God much more clearly and to sense his presence in a more tangible way. There are lots of Bible stories about watchmen waiting for the first rays of dawn to appear. As you walk, talk to each other and pray. Ask God to envision and equip you to 'rebuild the city walls'. Pray especially for the workers, who 'build' and establish the fabric of your local community. If you have picked up from someone in a prayer room before setting out, remember to hand over to the next person in your non-stop prayer chain before returning home for some well-earned rest.

PRAYING FOR WORKERS

Mobilise a team to conduct a series of one-off pastoral visits to church members in their workplaces during your prayer week.

These visits could double as 'soft' research about your local community (see Part 3) – team members can find out and record on paper the main issues which people in the workplace are facing. This would also be a good time to think beyond your prayer week and ask: 'What is God already doing in these workplaces?' and 'How can the church better equip its workers?'

Team members doing the visiting should remember to pray with those they visit, if possible. Also, the team should ideally gather together themselves before and after each series of visits to pray further for the workers concerned and about the issues or opportunities they have raised.

WHO THEN IS MY NEIGHBOUR?

A prayer poem by Mark Greene

Who then, Lord, is my neighbour?
For whom should I do some
time-consuming favour?
Spend some money from my not-exactly
arduous labour?
Is my neighbour so obviously abused?
Do all wounds that need healing necessarily
show a bruise?
Need it be something that makes
the ten o'clock news?

Who then is my neighbour?
I who rarely enter a danger zone
Or pass a stranger bleeding on their own.
Are there people I leave for dead:
Co-workers with griefs obvious
to the eye but left unsaid,
spouses who, you can tell, sleep chill
in their bed,
middle-aged men, waiting for the cull
that takes their head?

Are there people for whom no tears of mine
are shed:
new recruits whose golden zeal
has dulled to lead
60-hour-a-week cleaners whose kids
are not fully fed,
battered bosses trumpeting hope,
but living in dread?

Help me see, Lord, my neighbours
as you see
Help me love, Lord, as you have loved me.[13]

JUST BETWEEN YOU AND ME

A prayer poem by Mark Greene

> *Some things, I know, are better left unsaid,*
> *kept in the privacy of my own head,*
> *but just between you and me, Father*
> *I would really rather*
> *work for Attila the Hun*
> *than this arrogant, chauvinistic*
> *manipulative son of a gun,*
> *this bespoke-tailored stranger to the truth,*
> *this sexual predator, this paranoid pursuer*
> *of his lost youth…*
>
> *'Just between you and me'*
> * the Father began…*
>
> *…this incompetent, self-centred,*
> *self vaunting idolator of the great God I,*
> *snuffling for gold like a pig in a sty.*
>
> *'Just between you and me,' the Father said,*
> *'ponder this memo in the privacy of*
> * your head:*
>
> *One:*
> * when all you have to say is said*
> * and some of the things*
> * you are meant to have done*
> * are actually done*
> * note this: it is me that you work for,*
> * not that son of a gun.*
>
> *Two:*
> * all your charges may well be true,*
> * but do you really think that I love him*
> * any less than you?'*[14]

'BUSINESS OR BUSYNESS?'
– a journalling/writing exercise in two parts

Aim

The word 'business' can be heard in two different ways, either to mean work/profession or to have too much on your plate. This exercise challenges participants into evaluating both these aspects of their life and where God fits into it: to see your work as part of your faith and to encourage those who are too busy to slow down and take time out with God. This is an exercise for individuals. The instructions for each part could appear on a separate explanation card or alternatively on one big card. It would be useful to have a few copies in your prayer room so that more than one person can do it at a time.

Part 1: Business

It has been said that we either:

> work to live?
>
> – or –
>
> live to work?

- Do you agree with this statement? Why/why not?
- Which one do you identify with more – living to work or working to live?
- What about your colleagues and others you have contact with throughout the day?
- Are you satisfied with your response?
- If not, how would you like to change it?
- Do you feel that your work life, home life and church life are one and the same thing? Do you feel like you are the same person in these three aspects of your life? Or do you feel 'divided', that you are living a split personality life?
- If you feel like a 'split' person, does this bother you? Are you happy with the three defined parts?
- If not, why? And how can you change this?
- If yes, why? And what do you like about it?

Write your answers/response to God on paper, in the prayer room 'share' book or on the graffiti wall, if you have one.

Part 2: Busyness

The idea of Sabbath is sacred in the Bible. In essence, a Sabbath is about taking time out to be with God, getting to know God better, so you can live your life more in tune with him. Spend some time meditating on these psalms about being still and finding rest in God:

Psalm 5:3   Psalm 37:7   Psalm 46:10

Psalm 62:1   Psalm 84:2,10   Psalm 116:7-9

Then write a response prayer to God on your findings on paper, in the prayer room 'share' book or on the graffiti wall, if you have one.[15]

POP, FILM & TV 'TRIGGERS'
that you could use in a prayer event on the theme of business and employment:

I am a one in ten by UB40

Any songs about money – Beatles, Abba, Pink Floyd, Flying Lizards, Simply Red etc.

9 to 5 by Dolly Parton

Jerry McGuire

Wall Street

Only Fools and Horses

PRAYER POINTERS FOR BUSINESS AND EMPLOYMENT

- Hold an event to re-commission people in your church in paid or voluntary employment to be radical for God in their jobs.
- You could agree to pray regularly for, encourage and practically support people in the workplace.
- Open up your prayer room from 9-5 for local shop or office workers, making use of any contacts God has given you to publicise its availability by word of mouth or a small printed card.
- Run a week-long series of morning devotions about work for people on their way to work, or on their way home from it.

HOME AND OFFICE – A SENSORY PRAYER MEDITATION

God doesn't just speak to us 'in church' – he's in our workplaces, our homes and even our back gardens (if we are lucky enough to have one). This 'sensory' meditation teaches us to hear the voice of God through things we normally consider mundane.

Preparation

Before the event, prepare trays of objects. These can include anything you happen to have around your home, office, workplace or garden. For example, items from around your home could include paper, pen, pencil, sticky tape, eraser, screwdriver, torch, highlighter pen, lamp, glass, hammer, etc. – but the idea is easily adaptable to other environments. Make sure you have enough objects for everyone in each group.

Activity

Ask people to get into groups of six to eight. If you are using this idea for a small group, divide the people up only if you feel it is appropriate. When all groups are ready, place an object tray on the floor in the middle of each group. Inform them that you want them to reach out to God using one of these objects, listening to him for an encouraging word for someone in their group. Explain that you are not looking for directive words for anyone, but something that will build them up.

Once they have heard from God for someone else, encourage them to pick up the object and give it to the person before telling them what they received and praying for them. After they have finished, ask them to put the object back on the tray. Explain that the same object can be used more than once. Pray from the front for people's ears to be open to the living God. Explain how much time they have available to hear from God and give their word of encouragement. Experience shows that this activity can take twenty minutes or more to complete.

While they are reaching out to God and receiving words for each other, ask two or three of your leaders to go round the groups listening to see how they are getting on. If people have not started to give out their words, they should be encouraged to do so. If they are finding it difficult, the leader should stay with that group, answer their questions, reach out to God and show them by example how it is done.[16]

THE SPIRIT AT WORK – A SHORT BIBLICAL MEDITATION

A lot of the earliest followers of Jesus were business people. The apostle Paul, for example, made tents. A woman named Lydia traded expensive purple cloth. Zacchaeus was a tax man – who changed his corrupt business practices in response to Jesus' radical acceptance of him. The first Christians organised the distribution of food to needy widows every single day of the week (Acts 6:1). That's a lot of hard work, requiring efficient administration and probably a fair bit of business sense too. Interestingly, the job spec for this task called for people 'who are known to be full of the Spirit and wisdom' (Acts 6:3). From a kingdom perspective, intimacy with God through the Spirit is a necessary first requirement for those wanting to develop involvement in the practical needs of the community.

GET CONNECTED - BUSINESS AND EMPLOYMENT

Some Christian agencies that can support and inform you

LICC (The London Institute for Contemporary Christianity) works to equip Christians to engage biblically and relevantly with the issues they face, including work, capitalism, youth culture, media, gender and communication.

Tel: 0207 399 9555   Email: mail@licc.org.uk

Website: www.licc.org.uk / www.licc.org.uk/work

Stewardship is a Christian financial support services charity, committed to raising the standard of legal and financial administration in our churches and Christian organisations.

Tel: 08452 26 26 27   Email: enquiries@stewardship.org.uk

Website: www.stewardship.org.uk

Transformational Business Network (tbn) uses business to bring both spiritual and physical transformation to the world's poor.

Tel: 0845 330 5142   Email: info@tbnetwork.org

Website: www.tbnetwork.org

For books relating to business and employment, see the book lists in the Resources section at the back.

[12] From 'Towards the Conversion of England' 1945 – as quoted by LICC on http://www.licc.org.uk/article.php/id/1

[13] Mark Greene, *Pocket Prayers for Work*, (London: Church House Publishing, 2004)

[14] ibid.

[15] Blythe Toll and Gerard Kelly. Copyright 2004 The Bless Network (*www.bless.org.uk*)

[16] Adapted from Nancy Goudie's *Fifty Creative Worship Ideas – for the Whole Church and Small Groups*, (Eastbourne: Kingsway, 2002) p 89-90. www.nancygoudie.com

5 POLITICS, LAW AND ORDER

"SO THEY SAY ..."

He who shall introduce into public affairs the principles of primitive Christianity will change the face of the world.

Attributed to Benjamin Franklin

"SO THEY SAY ..."

Now Daniel so distinguished himself among the administrators and the satraps by his exceptional qualities that the king planned to set him over the whole kingdom.

Daniel 6:3

START HERE

Popular wisdom says that Christians and politics don't mix.

This says more about what politicians are perceived to be than it does about God's priorities. Politicians are seen to be those who cannot be trusted: those who only gain and keep power by devious and dubious means. But politics is – or should be – about running economies, caring for people. In other words, promoting justice and righteousness and caring for the poor, and God is passionate about these things.

Many characters in the Old Testament got involved in running the countries they lived in – Joseph, Daniel and Esther for a start. The prophets constantly cajoled the leaders to remember God's concerns for justice and righteousness (look at Amos and Hosea). And while Esther, Joseph and Daniel were not political leaders in the sense that we understand them today in a democracy – Joseph and Daniel were more like our civil servants – nevertheless they knew that God was concerned with the way people were governed. King David was described as a 'man after God's own heart' – and he was certainly a political leader.

What about Jesus? He didn't stage a political attack on the Romans, despite living under their occupation. So does that mean that he didn't think his disciples should be involved in politics? Again, we need to look at the bigger picture – did Jesus say anything that might make us think that God's agenda for people had changed, that caring for the poor and pursuing justice didn't matter any longer and evangelism was the only thing to go for? No. Luke 4:18-19 shows a wider concern than simply getting people to pray a prayer of salvation. Jesus constantly challenged injustice and corruption in his society – (Mk. 11:15-17, Mt. 23:23) and while the Romans may not have thought he threatened their power, the Pharisees and religious leaders did – and set out to destroy him as a result (Lk. 20:10).

The kingdom of God is about redeeming the whole of life and creation. We are commanded to pray for all our leaders – Christians, Muslims, atheists, agnostics or whoever – since they exercise power within God's creation:

> *I urge then, first of all, that requests, prayers, intercession and thanksgiving be made for everyone – for kings and all those in authority ...*

(1 Timothy 2:1)

Notice that it's not just good leaders we are meant to pray for. It's corrupt politicians too, it's dictatorial leaders and their advisors. It's even terrorists and those with illegitimate authority. We are meant to pray for all who influence society as a whole, and plead before God that they might, knowingly or unknowingly, come to be about God's work – promoting the good of the people, the saving of his world. Our *acceptance* of such leaders through prayer (the good, the bad and the ugly) doesn't mean that we necessarily *approve* of all their actions. Praying for them doesn't mean that we endorse every policy they create or the way they lead. Like us, they are imperfect. We are simply inviting God to step into our human affairs on the political level.

It's easy for us to throw stones at our politicians and other community leaders – but how about supporting them in the task through fervent prayer and engaging with them positively through united action? More and more, those in politics, law and order are open to working with faith-based groups, for the good of the whole community. There is a moment we can seize, and your prayer week is the ideal opportunity to start doing exactly that.

> *Father, turn us inside out; heads, hearts and lives. Give us a burning passion for justice, for mercy and for the well-being of our communities. Make us strong supporters of all that's right and good. Help us always to bless our leaders – locally, nationally and globally. Amen.*

POLITICS, LAW AND ORDER

THE BIBLE ON ... POLITICS, LAW AND ORDER

Based on Esther and Solomon – Esther 4 and 1 Kings 3

The stories of both Solomon and Esther, though from different times, are essentially about the same thing: faith, prayer and spirituality at work in the political arena.

Take Esther. She finds herself catapulted to prominence in the citadel of Susa, but at a time when the genocide of her own people is being plotted by the evil Haman. Her solution? Corporate fasting and courageous intervention – she gathers the Jews in Susa to pray and risks her life by approaching the king, uninvited.

Or take Solomon. Faced with God inviting him to ask for anything he wants, the king asks for nothing more than *wisdom* 'to govern this great people of yours'. (Of course, God promptly then gives him wealth beyond all his imagining – perhaps that's because Solomon has proved himself trustworthy?) Soon, in a legal dispute between two mothers over whose son was the dead son (and whose was alive), Solomon brings this heaven-sent wisdom into play in a spectacularly clever, landmark ruling. Solomon, for all his other faults, was one political leader who integrated his faith with his action, and his spirituality with his work.

Lord God, give us the courage of Esther and the wisdom of Solomon as we seek to integrate faith and action within our own political systems. Amen.

GEARING UP

Key questions to ask yourself/your church:

- Gather a list of all the people within your church community who work or volunteer in local or national political institutions, or in law and order.

- As a church community, what ways have you found actively to support these people and help them to work out their faith in this context?

- What more could you do as a church?

- What ways are you currently engaging, as a church community, with the political processes and institutions in your surrounding area, or in law and order?

- What more could you do? What ways can you serve, encourage, support and get involved in the processes of law and order or in local political groups in your surrounding area?

Key community sectors to consider engaging with:

- The police
- The probationary service
- Law firms and solicitors
- Your MP
- Local councillors
- Local HQs of political parties

INTIMACY AND INVOLVEMENT

Real-life Stories of Faith in Action

INSIDE THE MAZE OF PARLIAMENTARY POLITICS

Jo Holland is a Parliamentary Researcher for the Liberal Democrat Member of Parliament, Steve Webb.

I first visited Parliament as a sixth former with my A-level politics class, and remember being delighted at getting a glimpse of what went on behind the millions of windows of the most famous landmark in London. I never suspected that, five years later, I would actually be working behind one of those windows!

The maze of corridors, staircases and passageways inside the Palace of Westminster meant that it took me a week before I could find my office without asking for directions. Even now, several years later, I am amazed at how easy it is to get lost in the bowels of this huge and elegant building!

I am addicted to the variety and the buzz of the place. It is very exciting to see how policies are made and agendas are shaped within these walls – and to play a part in making and shaping them. My work ranges from providing briefings for speeches and assisting with policy formation, to taking constituents on tours of Parliament and making sure that the office runs smoothly each day. There is rarely a dull moment. One of the most fulfilling parts of my job is supporting my Christian boss in his role as an MP, and praying for and within Parliament as part of a cross-party group of Christian staff.

A real hunger to pray for Parliament has been growing within many of the Christians who work here, and last year's Alpha course and 24/7 Prayer week both really inspired us to seek God's will here in a new and deeper way. We don't yet know where this will lead us, but we are increasingly excited about God's plans for this place, and seek to be faithful in prayer until they are revealed.

My aim as a Parliamentary researcher is to be salt and light in every task – from the formation of policy ideas to daily interaction with my colleagues, and to reflect the love of Christ in this tough environment. In the cut-and-thrust world of party politics, people notice if you live by a different set of rules. That is the main challenge for me and my Christian colleagues here – to live differently and to prompt people to ask 'Why?'

CREATIVE PRAYER

IDEAS AND RESOURCES FOR YOUR PRAYER WEEK

LOCAL COUNCILLORS

Decide in your homegroup, youth group, church or other group to gather together and pray for your local councillors each week for a month. Ask God to give them wisdom to govern well. Confess that all too often we neglect to pray for those in local government – except at election time! As God's people, corporately offer your hands, hearts, feet, minds, voices and time to him, and make yourselves available (as Isaiah did) – should he choose to send you into that sphere of influence.

> Then I heard the voice of the Lord saying, 'Whom shall I send? And who will go for us?' And I said, 'Here am I. Send me!'

(Isaiah 6:8)

THE LAYING ON OF HANDS (BUT IN A FRIENDLY WAY)

Invite any lawyers, police officers or others in the realm of law and order to give a ten-minute talk on how being a Christian there makes a difference to their faith and their work. At the end, physically gather around those who have shared, laying hands on them (gently, we mean – after all, they are the strong arm of the Law!) and praying for God to empower and inspire them to be a beacon of light in their field of work.

VISIT YOUR MP OR MAJOR POLITICAL INSTITUTIONS

Visit your MP in their constituency surgery as part of your preparation for your prayer week and ask for their top five local problems or needs, to incorporate in the prayer life of your church ahead of time.

If you live close to a Parliament or a regional assembly, arrange for members of your group to visit, in order to learn about current political issues and start praying about them.

POP, FILM AND TV 'TRIGGERS'

that you could use in a prayer event on the theme of politics, law and order:

Like a king by Ben Harper

I fought the law by The Clash

For what it's worth by Buffalo Springfield

The West Wing

The Bill

The John Grisham films – *The Firm, The Client, The Pelican Brief, The Rainmaker*

Twelve Angry Men

Changing Lanes

Dave

Yes Minister

Inspector Morse

Robin Hood Prince of Thieves

A Few Good Men

Bowling for Columbine

GO AND DO THIS ... ACTIVE PRAYER

Make contact with your local police station and with one or more of your local 'bobbies-on-the-beat'. (Of course, perhaps you already have a police officer in your congregation in which case that part is easy.) Explain that your church is keen to be kept up-to-date with needs of the local community – and to support it both in terms of prayer and work wherever possible. Ask if you can accompany one or more police officers on the beat, for them to show you the areas of greatest need. You'll probably be amazed, and possibly depressed, by what they show you.

If things go well, a further development of this idea might be to take a group round to your local police station, or on another local walkabout, to envision and enthuse people about getting involved in community policing for themselves. Alternatively, why not consider inviting some of your local police officers to speak at your church in an informal setting?

GLOBAL POLITICAL ACTIVITY

Aim

To encourage participants to think about global political issues and what their response should be as a Christian. 1 Timothy 2:1-2 is a good starting point for exploring this idea in Scripture. It's a good idea to display this verse somewhere in the room, for people to see, pray and meditate on as they come to your prayer event.

Materials required

Letter-writing pack

Pens/paper

Envelopes/stamps

Post box

Instructions

Get some letter-writing packs from one of the organisations listed below. These packs provide information on pressing issues and tips on how to write letters. Each participant can write a letter on whatever issue is most pressing to them. Supply envelopes and stamps and create a letterbox where they can 'post' the letter once they have written it.[17]

---

[17] Blythe Toll and Gerard Kelly. Copyright 2004 The Bless Network (*www.bless.org.uk*)

GET CONNECTED – POLITICS, LAW AND ORDER

Some Christian agencies that can support and inform you

CARE is a Christian charity involved in caring, campaigning and communicating across the UK, seeking to combine practical caring initiatives with public policy on social and ethical issues.
Tel: 020 7233 0455   Email: communications@care.org.uk
Website: www.care.org.uk

Christians In Politics is a joint initiative of the recognised Christian groups in the Conservative, Labour and Liberal Democrat parties. It exists to encourage more Christians – and other people of goodwill, committed to the common good – into public life.
Tel: 020 8786 9095   Email: mail@christiansinpolitics.fsnet.co.uk
Website: www.christiansinpolitics.org.uk

Christian Solidarity Worldwide (CSW) is a human rights organisation specialising in religious freedom. CSW works on behalf of those persecuted for their Christian beliefs and promotes religious liberty for all.
Tel: 0208 942 8810   Email: admin@csw.org.uk
Website: www.csw.org.uk

Faithworks exists to empower and inspire individual Christians and every local church to develop their role at the hub of their community. In the political arena, Faithworks speaks to both central and local government about the extraordinary impact of the Church in addressing the needs of UK society today.
Tel: 020 7450 9071   Email: info@faithworks.info
Website: www.faithworks.info

Jubilee Campaign are a human rights pressure group, lobbying to protect children's rights and the persecuted church.
Tel: 01483 894787   Email: info@jubileecampaign.co.uk
Website: www.jubileecampaign.co.uk

Open Doors minister to persecuted Christians worldwide, providing them with Bibles and other Christian literature, leadership and pastoral training, community development schemes, prayer and personal encouragement.
Tel: 01993 885400   Email: info@opendoorsuk.org
Website: www.opendoorsuk.org

Books relating to politics, law and order can be found in the book lists in the Resources section at the back.

6 THE EXCLUDED ...

"SO THEY SAY ..."

*As the purse is emptied,
the heart is filled.*

Victor Hugo

"SO THEY SAY ..."

*Accustom yourself continually to
make many acts of love, for they
enkindle and melt the soul.'*

St Teresa of Avila

"SO THEY SAY ..."

*The church can support professionals
who work among the excluded by
being there, not by criticising from a
distance. How about offering one-to-
one mentoring to those who want it?*

Annie Turner, CEO, *The Big Issue*

IDEAS AND RESOURCES FOR YOUR PRAYER WEEK

START HERE

Despite starting as a dynamic organism, a living 'body' of people that spilled out onto the streets moments after it was born in the upper room, the global church to which we belong can all too easily become no more than an organisation with four walls and a weekly hymn sandwich. It's sad, but often true.

But if there was a theme during our prayer weeks to bring us back to reality, back to integrated faith, and back to life, it's the excluded. Follow in Jesus' footsteps around your town – whether it's Grimsby, Glasgow or Glastonbury – and search for those on the fringe. Live out on the edge to find those who have no choice but to live on the edge. Feel God's heart for the excluded, the disadvantaged, the broken and the despairing. Bring hope to the hurting and new life to the dead.

And as you pray, don't just ask for change in someone else's situation, but ask for the transformation of your own heart, mind and inner life.

The church is the largest voluntary body by far in the UK. Local communities and national government know that if the church went on strike tomorrow, there would be a very large bill to pay to cover a massive shortfall in social provision, not least in the astonishing amount of youth work done by churches up and down the country.

So let's not kid ourselves that as God's people, we're doing nothing. Nor that, overnight, we can do everything. However, your prayer week and the months that follow are prime time to hear the Creator's heartbeat for the forgotten. Make the most of the opportunity to reach out to the marginalised, the invisible and the forgotten.

THE BIBLE ON ... THE EXCLUDED

Based on Luke and other gospel accounts

IDEAS AND RESOURCES FOR YOUR PRAYER WEEK

Jesus touches a leper. Jesus receives attention from a prostitute. Jesus forgives and heals a blind 'sinner'. Jesus spends time with a Samaritan woman. Jesus blesses children. Jesus visits Zacchaeus, a taxman. Each of these simple acts of blessing and acceptance created massive shockwaves in the culture of Jesus' time.

Lepers, for instance, were thought to be unclean. Prostitutes were known to be. It was thought that the blind were disabled because of sin in the family. Samaritans and women were second-class citizens. Children didn't matter – remember the disciples' attitude when Jesus wanted to bless the children? Taxmen were traitors to the rest of the Jewish community.

We need only to scratch at the surface of Luke's gospel and there are crowds and crowds of broken and excluded people, running into the arms of the one person in human history who refuses to judge or condemn them.

Will we be remembered as a narrow-minded, elusive and exclusive people? Or as a church that embraces all people with the same grace that's been extended to us?

Thank God for the many examples down through the ages of Christians who have spent themselves on behalf of the poor and needy. Pray for the ability to follow in their footsteps, offering dignity and hope to those who are poor in spirit.

GEARING UP

Key questions to ask yourself/your church:

- Gather a list of all the people within your church community who work (full or part time) or volunteer in projects that serve people on the margins of society, people often described as excluded (e.g. refugees/asylum seekers, rough sleepers, unemployed people, people with disabilities, etc.).

- As a church community, what ways have you found actively to support these people, and help them to work out their faith in that context?

- What more could you do as a church?

- What ways are you currently engaging, *as a church community*, with those described as excluded in your surrounding community?

- What more could you do in the wider community? What ways can you serve, encourage and support local authority and social services projects, voluntary projects and those run by other churches? You might need to do a bit of research to answer this fully.

- Are you aware of any gaps (your research may reveal some) where needs are not being met? Pray. Maybe God is speaking to your church community about starting something new to meet these needs?

Key community sectors to consider engaging with:

- Prison communities
- Homeless people and those serving them
- Ethnic minority groups
- Disability groups
- The elderly
- Any other marginalised or stigmatised group – be the first to open a line of communication, support and hope
- Really the list is almost endless …

INTIMACY AND INVOLVEMENT

Real-life Stories of Faith in Action

PRAYING ON YOUR FEET (LITERALLY)

My name is Helen Newman and I'm 26. I work with Young Unaccompanied Asylum Seekers/Refugees (ages 16-19ish!) as an Outreach Support Officer.

I see these young people and how little they have, not just in terms of 'material things', but also their lack of role models, of people who really care and I want to make a difference.

I love this job because it allows me to make a small but real difference in their lives. Many young refugees and asylum seekers have experienced terrible atrocities and are now just barely surviving. In my job, I get opportunities to encourage them and help them to succeed in small things, and I hope that through this I can play a small part in their healing.

Having said that, sympathy itself will not heal them, and encouragement alone will not help them see what they can achieve, and nor will these give them status to stay in the UK. They need something more than I can give. I heard Pete Greig speak at a 24-7 Prayer day in 2002 – he urged us to 'keep on praying', to persevere. I felt my heart breaking. After months wondering if I should quit my job, not knowing how to challenge or change some of the injustices and frustration, I felt God speak to me and inspire me.

Since then, I've been learning to pray all the things I want for these young people – they have little hope, so I hope for them and dream for them, and pray for them. One of my friends even suggested that I write my prayers on my feet every day so that they 'go to work' with me, so that's what I've been doing recently. I pray when I meet with my young people, when they have court appeals, when they invite me into their home and bless me without knowing. I help in whatever way I can, trying to let them know that they are special and important, I try to be like Jesus in those moments. I'm no expert, but Jesus doesn't expect me to be one.

CREATIVE PRAYER

GO AND DO THIS ... ACTIVE PRAYER: CANDLELIT VIGIL

Find the most public outdoor place in your town and take a group to hold a simple, candlelit vigil there for the excluded. Avoid doing anything that would fit the Christian stereotype. That means guitars, open-air preaching and arm-twisting evangelistic conversations are all out! Instead, aim to provoke questions by lighting numerous small tealights (guard well against any fire risk). When people start asking what all the candles are for, tell them it's a meditation or protest or prayer gathering for the excluded. At that point, and only then, offer them a postcard or business card with details of your prayer room, inviting them to pay a visit. Make sure you give advance warning to nearby shops, the police and the local authority of your vigil. Remember, even your preparation for such an event is an opportunity to grow positive, local friendships.

GET YOUR HANDS DIRTY

This sensory meditation is all about touch. Not to mention mission, sacrifice and hard work too! It can easily be adapted as one feature of your prayer room if you wish, reminding us all that a hurting world is waiting for kingdom people who will really get stuck in ...

Preparation

You will need a bag of clean compost – enough for everyone to take a handful. Put the bag at the front of the venue with old newspapers or a plastic cover underneath so it is easy to clear up later.

Activity

At the beginning, before your event or talk, ask people to come forward and take a handful of soil. Ask them to rub their hands in the dirt and then go back to their seats. Then talk about the importance of getting our hands dirty for God.

During your talk or event, ask how many people would like to be able to wash their hands and feel clean again. Probably a lot would say that this was the case. Explain that when we get involved in kingdom business, we will often get our hands dirty, and therefore at times we will want to wash our hands of what is going on. However, in order to see the kingdom established, it is important that we keep going and do not give up – even if it is uncomfortable for us. Emphasise that it would be far easier for us just to give up and wash our hands but God wants to encourage us to keep on going and see the work through.[18]

POP, FILM AND TV 'TRIGGERS'

that you could use in a prayer event on the theme of the excluded:

Beautiful by Christina Aguilera

So lonely by The Police

Across the lines by Tracy Chapman

Peace on earth by U2

Martin Luther King's 'I have a dream' speech[19]

Philadelphia (HIV)

Amistad (anti-slavery)

Chocolat (the gypsy community)

She's All That

About A Boy

Dead Man Walking

The Shawshank Redemption

A Beautiful Mind

GO AND DO THIS … ACTIVE PRAYER: THE 'INVISIBLES'

Take a walk and look out for the 'invisible' people in your community. These are the people we are normally too busy to notice. Those like blind Bartimaeus on the roadside, or Zacchaeus up a tree, that Jesus was happy to be distracted by. Go at different times of the day with a friend – early morning, midday, late afternoon, at dusk or late at night. Search for elderly faces in the windows, the lonely sitting on a park bench, the single parent, people selling *The Big Issue*, the men in pubs or betting shops and so on.

- If you're feeling brave, start a conversation with someone you would normally walk past.

- Ask God to show you even more 'invisible' people than you could ever see with just your natural eyes.

- When you meet excluded people, remember that one of the most powerful and precious things you can do for them is simply to look into their eyes, listen to them, be with them, and thereby begin to restore their dignity and self-esteem.

- Ask him to give you a burning compassion for excluded people.

CIRCLE OF INCLUSION ACTIVITY

Aim

To provoke thoughts on what exclusion really means. The idea of exclusion can often be quite a cliché in our churches. But perhaps we have missed the point of exclusion and what it means, and who we have or have not excluded.

Decoration of the room

Fill the prayer room with images of what it means to be 'excluded.' You can do this by using OHP slides and photocopied images on transparencies. Try and think laterally about this, as the idea of excluded people can often be stereotyped. Obvious images would be of starving children in Africa; homeless or drug addicted teenagers; old people etc. But what about considering some well respected people that might be excluded – businessmen or pastors etc. A helpful question in thinking about what images to use could be: 'People excluded from what?' Think of some possible scenarios people could be excluded from and find images relating to that.

In the centre of the room, create a large circle using a piece of string or rope. After participants have had time to explore the notions of the excluded in their community etc., they can come and spend some time praying or meditating and offering their lives to God, while sitting in the circle. A circle is a symbol of inclusion. So the bigger the circle the better – as more people can be included within it.

This is a chance for participants to realise that although they may have felt excluded from the community or society, God does not exclude them. It might even be helpful to encourage participants to think about being in the same circle or sitting next to those people whom they like to exclude and challenge them to bring those thoughts and feelings to God. If you have a projector, why not project an image down into the centre of circle. It could either be an image representing inclusion, just the word inclusion, or a Bible verse.

You may find it helpful to print a short explanation card for each participant, something like the one below.[20]

Explanation card

Once you have explored the idea of exclusion and perhaps your part in excluding others, or being excluded yourself, come and enter the circle, and sit/stand/kneel/lie in the middle of the room. A circle is a powerful image of inclusion. As you enter the circle, realise that no matter how excluded you may have felt in the past, you are included in God's plan and love! Remember though, God really doesn't have any boundaries; his 'circle' is so wide that we cannot find the edge of it. Are there people or have there been people that you have excluded in the past? As you sit in the circle, visualise them in the circle, sitting next to you. How does this make you feel? Ask God to help you see that they are just as included in his plan, as you are, and to give you the strength and ability to include them in the future.

GET CONNECTED - THE EXCLUDED ...

Some Christian agencies that can support and inform you

Caritas – Social Action seeks to promote Catholic social action within the church and in society as a whole.
Tel: 020 7901 4875   Email: caritas@cbcew.org.uk
Website: www.caritas-socialaction.org.uk

Credit Action is a national money education charity committed to helping people manage their money better. Its passion is to help people stay in control, rather than let money control them and disrupt their lives through over indebtedness.
Tel: 01522 699777   Email: office@creditaction.org.uk
Website: www.creditaction.org.uk

OAS!S Trust is committed to demonstrating the Christian faith in action. It works in communities across the world, seeking to provide holistic solutions to the major social issues of our time.
Tel: 020 7450 9000   Email: enquiries@oasistrust.org
Website: www.oasistrust.org

Shaftesbury Housing Group is a leading Christian Registered Social Landlord (Housing Association) and substantial provider of affordable housing, residential care and support services for over 25,000 people.
Tel: 01372 727252   Email: info@shaftesburyhousing.org.uk
Website: www.shaftesburyhousing.org.uk

YMCAs are Christian charities belonging to a national and worldwide movement which are committed to meeting the needs of young people regardless of their gender, race, ability, age or faith. They offer young people and their communities opportunities to develop in mind, body and spirit and so fulfil their potential.
Tel: 020 8520 5599   Email: enquiries@ymca.org.uk
Website: www.ymca.org.uk

[18] Adapted from Nancy Goudie's *Fifty Creative Worship Ideas – for the Whole Church and Small Groups*, (Eastbourne: Kingsway, 2002) p 55-56. www.nancygoudie.com

[19] This can be found via Google, under 'I have a dream.'

[20] Adapted from material supplied by Blythe Toll and Gerard Kelly. Copyright 2004 The Bless Network (*www.bless.org.uk*)

FINALE EVENT

A commissioning service for local community engagement

The grand finale to your prayer week should be a commissioning service where you make a big deal about encouraging people to share their stories about what God has been doing through the prayer room during the seven previous days.

Your commissioning service, whether on a Sunday or another day of the week, is also an ideal opportunity to sign the Faithworks Charter, which contains well thought-through and worked-through principles which every church can aspire to as part of their community engagement.[21]

This service or event is the moment when all that Upper Room prayer activity begins to swing into outward and 'out-worked' mission. So, while you are celebrating the successful completion of 168 hours of non-stop prayer (or near enough), keep one eye and one ear out for where you suspect God is taking you, your church, your family, your friends and your workplaces, next.

PENTECOST PURPOSE

Written by Steve Chalke, based on Acts 2:1-14

Pentecost Sunday marks the birthday of the church – the moment when Christ's followers are empowered for the task of mission that lay ahead of them. Jesus said to them 'Wait here until the Spirit comes on you … then you will be my witnesses in Jerusalem, Judea, Samaria and to the ends of the Earth.' Then in Acts 2 Luke tells us the story of how God poured his Spirit out on ordinary men and women for just that reason.

WHO DOES GOD CHOOSE TO POUR HIS SPIRIT ON?

It is often said that Pentecost marks the moment in history when God first pours his Spirit out on people. But the real significance of Pentecost is something very different.

There are numerous occasions in the Old Testament where we are told that God's Spirit fills a particular individual for a specific task. Throughout the Old Testament God's Spirit falls on their chosen leaders. For instance … Saul, David, Moses, Deborah, Joshua. So the idea of God's Spirit filling a human being is nothing new. The difference however is this: In the Old Testament all that the 'ordinary' people get to do is stand back, marvel and watch!

But on the day of Pentecost we see something entirely new. As Peter puts it, quoting the prophet Joel, 'In the last days I will pour out my Spirit on all people' – young and old, male and female (see Acts 2:17). So to the question: Who gets filled with God's Spirit? The answer is: Everyone – the ordinary people, not just the leaders. Or to put it another way … if you are willing, you do! This is the good news of the gospel. We are not just forgiven, it is even better than that. God chooses to use us. He chooses to use you.

WHY DOES GOD CHOOSE TO POUR HIS SPIRIT OUT?

When the Holy Spirit fell on Jesus' followers they all 'began to speak in other tongues as the Spirit enabled them' (Acts 2:4). But why the gift of speaking in tongues? Over the years the 'gift of tongues' has proved to be utterly contentious. So why does God grant this and not some other, less controversial, gift?

In Matthew 28 Jesus sets out for his followers his radical agenda, or what we now call the Great Commission. Their task was to go to all *nations* and make disciples.

But the word *ethnos*, which we have translated as nation, is more accurately translated *ethnic group,* or even *tribe.* In other words it defines people by their language, customs, beliefs, morals, values and culture rather than by their country of residence. Jesus is calling his followers to take the issue of ethnicity and situation seriously and to work with and respect it rather than be blind to it or attempt to ignore it.

It is this principle that is underlined in Acts 2 when, on receiving the Holy Spirit, the same disciples are given the ability to 'speak in tongues'. These are not, however, the heavenly languages that the church has so often argued about over the centuries. How do we know? Because verses 5 and 6 make it absolutely clear. It explains that there were, staying in Jerusalem, 'Jews from every nation under heaven' and that when Jesus' disciples began to speak in other tongues their response was 'Are not all these men who are speaking Galileans? Then how is it that each of us hears them in our own native language?' (Acts 2:7-8).

The disciples found themselves speaking in the individual dialects or mother tongues of those different groups of Jews gathered together in Jerusalem for Pentecost. God's vision clearly takes diversity seriously and affirms, not obliterates, the obvious differences of those present.

Jesus' intent was never to see a homogeneous society or church. And when Paul later writes that there is now neither Jew nor Gentile (Gal. 3:28) he is not reinterpreting the teachings of Jesus in a subtle attempt to move towards a kind of *one-size-fits-all church*. Indeed, at the beginning of his letter he has already taken issue with Peter and the Jerusalem church over their attempts to make the Gentiles adopt Jewish customs. Paul understood that the way forward was diversity under a shared vision – not an insipid uniformity. His was a multicultural vision more akin to a fruit salad, where the distinctions remain and are celebrated, rather than being obliterated in a bland puree where everyone is forced to lose their identity to belong.

The church must be committed to mission and evangelism which takes race, language and culture seriously and to serving in ways where diversity is encouraged, not squashed. But here is the twist. All those who had gathered in Jerusalem on that day could speak the same language. How do we know that? Because they were all Jews. They all understood Hebrew and, on top of that, would also have had a working knowledge of Greek – the official language of the Roman Empire! So there were two perfectly good 'global' languages that the disciples were naturally fluent in that could have been used to communicate to the crowds that day.

Therefore, perhaps the greatest miracle of Pentecost is this – that what happens demonstrates that God's choice is to speak to us in our own languages. He begins where we are. He comes to us. He does not treat those assembled as 'a crowd' but instead as individuals. They hear the good news in their own language. God comes to meet them using the words that they learned on their mother's knee – that they thought in and dreamt in.

Jesus' life – the incarnation – is all about the fact that God came to us, became one of us and spoke our language. He accommodated himself to us. Here, on the day of Pentecost, he miraculously equips the church to do the same. And the rest of the contents of the book of Acts is the story of how the first Christians begin to work out what it means to do just that on a day-to-day basis, discovering what it means to contextualise the gospel for each people group. (See how Paul does this in Athens in Acts 17:16-31.)

That remains the task of the church today – to start where people are; to get involved in our communities; to 'speak their language'. To go to them, not wait for them to come to us. It is for this purpose that God gives his Spirit.

WHEN DOES GOD CHOOSE TO POUR HIS SPIRIT OUT?

What were all these Jews from around the known world doing in Jerusalem in the first place? What was Pentecost? Pentecost was part of the historic Jewish harvest festival. Seven full weeks (49 days) after the grain harvest, the people were to bring a 'freewill' offering to the Lord. This was known as the feast of Weeks or Pentecost, referring to the fiftieth day: (see Deut. 16:9-10). So those who had gathered in the city on that day were there to bring their offerings to the Temple and to celebrate God's goodness to them. These people were in Jerusalem to present the best of their harvest; the work of their hands back to God in thanksgiving to him.

And it is in this context that God pours out his Spirit, first on the apostles and then on all those who cry out to him. Once again, as Peter reminds the crowd, God says 'I will pour out my Spirit on all people'. And it is still that way today. As we bring ourselves to God, graciously he chooses to fill us with his Spirit and power for the task of mission and engagement. He doesn't ask us to bring what we don't have. He never seeks to compare and contrast us with others. He simply asks us to bring our best. And it is in that moment that he pours out his Spirit on us, his people.

Prayerworks: Part 2

Jon Harris

Dave Hitchcock

[21] For a full copy of this Charter, turn to the end of Part 3

PART 3:

THE FAITHWORKS SEVEN STEP GUIDE TO ACTION

Introduction

The Faithworks Seven Step Guide To Action

Step 1: Big oaks from little acorns grow – finding ideas and inspiration

Step 2: Do your homework – the importance of preparation

Step 3: What's in the cupboard? – assessing your resources

Step 4: Don't hide your light! – being distinctively Christian

Step 5: Pounds, planning and pence – creating a business plan and budget

Step 6: Paper and money – top tips for obtaining funding

Step 7: Together is better – working in partnership with others

Joining the Faithworks Movement

Faithworks Awards

Faithworks Conference

Faithworks Membership

Faithworks Affiliation

Faithworks Local Networks

The Faithworks Charter

INTRODUCTION

It's Pentecost, and the disciples have been praying night and day. Peter the apostle stands up and delivers a sparkling, well-prepared sermon. When he finishes, thousands respond to his altar call – 'Repent and be baptised!' – and the band begins to play … Right? Well, not entirely.

Peter's preaching is actually more like a hastily-arranged press conference. It's a question and answer session given in response to the Holy Spirit invading the upper room and those praying within it. Far from being polished or rehearsed, his message is a short, unscripted, public broadcast. God is speaking through the disciples to Jews from all over the ancient world in their own mother tongues – to each one in the language they can best understand. Peter, meanwhile, is simply responding to questions from the growing crowd which has assembled in bewilderment at this divinely orchestrated spectacle.

Specifically, there are two questions everyone is asking: 'What does this mean?' (Acts 2:12) and, soon after, 'Brothers, what shall we do?' (Acts 2:37).

'What does this mean?' and 'What shall we do?' are two questions that every Prayerworks week is designed to prompt. It may not be that your group starts simultaneously speaking a foreign language. But it could be that a twelve-year-old child prophesies and your whole church responds: 'God is speaking to us.' Or it could be that a window of opportunity opens to meet an urgent need in the community. Or that the same crazy idea occurs to three people independently while they are brushing their teeth on a Tuesday morning. Or … it could be something else entirely. When God answers prayer, he often does it in surprising and unique ways that may initially bemuse us, then amaze us, but which finally lead us to change and to do something different: to put our faith to work. As you are finishing your 24-7 Prayer session, don't be surprised to find people in your community wondering out loud:

WHAT DO WE DO NEXT?

It's clear from the Pentecost story that the answer to this question involves repentance (Acts 2:38). Repentance, though, is much more than a momentary nod in heaven's direction. If we read on, we see it's actually all about a changed lifestyle (2:42-47), one that involves nothing less than *all* of who we are and *all* of what we have.

> *Selling their possessions and goods, they gave to anyone as he had need.*
>
> (Acts 2:45)

This is a lifestyle of radical and selfless commitment to hands-on, practical service. It sounds demanding because it is demanding. But don't worry: at this point on the curve, somewhere between praying and doing, Faithworks can help you to begin to put 'hands and feet' on the many prayers you have prayed over the last few days:

- Faithworks exists to empower and inspire individual Christians and local churches to develop their role at the hub of their community.
- Faithworks aims to challenge and change the public perception of the church by engaging with the media and government.
- Faithworks encourages churches and individual Christians to work together and, in partnership with other groups, to deliver effective services in the local community.

This part of *Prayerworks* explains how your church, group or organisation can be empowered, resourced and equipped for local community involvement. But before you rush to set up your dream community project, you might want to consider a wider variety of options:

- Take a group on a 24-7 Mission team – maybe your prayer participants got inspired by the concept of 24-7 mission? Visit www.24-7mission.com to find out more.
- Identify and support the professionals in your congregation – parents, teachers, lawyers, police officers, social workers etc. This is a very good place to start in your local mission.
- Sign the Faithworks Charter – and do remember, the Charter is aspirational, something to think through carefully and work towards, not just a piece of paper to sign and file somewhere safe, nor a stick to beat yourselves up with!
- Do more 24-7 Prayer – it could be that you feel you should wait a while, give 24-7 Prayer a second or third go, and steadily make it more outward-focused. This is how most Boiler Rooms (permanent 24-7-365 creative/prayer/mission communities) get started.

However you and your group are feeling after your burst of non-stop prayer (apart from tired?!), don't avoid reading this 'doing' or 'mission' bit of *Prayerworks* just because it seems hard. The joy of putting prayer and faith to work far outweighs the pain and sacrifice. So … get stuck in, and you may well surprise yourself, your church and your local community with what is achieved.

Whether you want to set up a community project right away, or are considering one of the other options outlined above, there are lots of different resources here that will help with the onward journey. Turn to the later sections for information on Faithworks awards, conference, affiliation, local networks and much more.

Whatever you decide to do, don't hold back – go for it with a passion!

THE FAITHWORKS SEVEN STEP GUIDE TO ACTION

THE FAITHWORKS SEVEN STEP GUIDE TO ACTION

Maybe you *have* just left the prayer room with an idea for a project that will transform the world, or at least St Winifred's parish, Anytown, and the 'worlds' of those within it. Now is the time to recognise that there may be a great deal of work ahead. You'll need friends for the journey, and also some clear thinking, sound strategy, detailed plans and (above all) Heaven's help, for the challenging and rewarding days ahead.

To give you the best possible start in your community initiative, here's a seven step guide from Faithworks to help you start putting your idea into action. During each step, you'll find lots of different resources offered to inspire and equip you. Even if you're not yet setting up a project, there's plenty in these pages to help you to start taking action on a smaller scale.

STEP 1: BIG OAKS FROM LITTLE ACORNS GROW
– FINDING IDEAS AND INSPIRATION

It's easy to get discouraged if we focus on the large, obviously successful projects – but that is a mistake; we should be focusing on the people we need to help. Even the tallest trees grow from a small seed.

STEVE CHALKE

Ideas and inspiration can come from almost anywhere. It might be from an extraordinary experience or an ordinary circumstance. God uses both. It could be angels, dreams, divine confirmation or supernatural provision. Or it could be through books, music, nature, television, parties, train journeys, the bath or sitting outside your child's nursery. Most likely, it will be a combination of all these things. If you are waiting for inspiration, take the opportunity to learn to listen to God in ways that are different to those you are familiar with.

Theresa gets inspired by Bengali mothers

Theresa sat outside her child's nursery class watching the two Bengali mothers looking at a children's reading book. She had seen them plenty of times before, struggling to understand the childish English, but today she felt they needed extra help. She moved over, sat between them and began to explain the simple words. Within a month, her first lesson had turned into a regular class in one of the mothers' homes. Within eighteen months she had an organisation, 'Open Doors', with numerous teachers, which partnered with the local authority and which was even invited to give lessons in the local mosque.

Philip gets inspired by an angel

Now an angel of the Lord said to Philip "Go south to the road – the desert road – that goes down from Jerusalem to Gaza." So he started out, and on his way he met an Ethiopian eunuch, an important official in charge of all the treasury ... He was sitting in his chariot reading the book of Isaiah the prophet. The Spirit told Philip, "Go to that chariot and stay near it." Then Philip ran up to the chariot.

(Acts 8:26-29)

Philip didn't just get the idea to go for a walk along the desert road, he responded to an angel, to the Spirit of God. We may not often hear angels in our prayer times, but God does speak to us, through his word, through ordinary means such as circumstances and other people, and through not-so-ordinary ways. And it is often during times of extended prayer that we are able to hear him most clearly.

But how do we respond? Philip's obedient and decisive response meant that he was in the right place at the right time, which happened to be running alongside a moving chariot on a desert road. The eunuch understood the Scriptures, believed, repented and was baptised, and the Gospel began to spread out beyond Jerusalem.

Paul gets inspired by a Macedonian man

During the night Paul had a vision of a man of Macedonia standing and begging him, "Come over to Macedonia and help us." After Paul had seen the vision, we got ready at once to leave for Macedonia, concluding that God had called us to preach the gospel to them.

(Acts 16:9,10)

That vision and the way Paul acted immediately to follow God's word was the start of the important work in taking Christianity to modern-day Europe and beyond. If he hadn't said 'Yes' to God, there might have been no miraculous release from prison, no debate at the Areopagus in Athens and no sending the word of God to Corinth, where Paul stayed for eighteen months. The book of Acts could have ended up much thinner!

I'm stuck for inspiration

Of course, sometimes it's hard to know where to start. But if you're stuck for inspiration, why not:

- Flick back through the 'prayer-log' from your week of prayer and see what local needs keep surfacing in the prayer life of your group. These might be a good place to start working, since people are already clearly passionate about praying for them!
- Get hold of *100 Proven Ways to Transform Your Community*. This Faithworks book outlines one hundred different projects, some big schemes running into millions of pounds, and others much smaller and simpler, that are a proven success in their local communities.

Speakers

Invite someone who works in a particular field of expertise – education, politics, for example – to visit your church, and ask them to get you thinking about what you can do practically in your community.

Online information directory

www.faithworks.info/directory covers all major areas of community involvement. Browse through the subjects from addiction, through housing and homelessness, to youth work. It is a mine of fantastic information, which will help you decide which area you can work in.

STEP 2: DO YOUR HOMEWORK
– THE IMPORTANCE OF PREPARATION

Read, mark, learn and inwardly digest.

THE BOOK OF COMMON PRAYER

I began by researching the local area to find out what was going on. I arrived ready to change the world, but for three months I simply visited local schools, families and the local library to chat to people there in order to build my information about the area. At the time it was incredibly frustrating, but as I look back now, I am very grateful for it.

PAUL SANDERSON, THE WIRE PROJECT, LITTLEHAMPTON

Here's a question: what was Jesus doing for thirty years before he launched his public ministry? We don't know for sure, but a good guess would be… *preparation*. He was getting ready for an explosive three year period of ministry that would rock the world. The Father knew that his Son, a human being like any of us, had to learn to walk, to talk, to question, to grow, to live, to be educated and to learn some of life's harder lessons – in order to be fully ready for the challenges ahead. Thirty years of preparation might sound wasteful, but if Jesus took the time and effort, shouldn't we…?

We need to get ready if we are to offer people around us the best chance of hope. A good example of this is The Wire Project. This was set up to put life back into Wick, a town of seven thousand people on the South Downs, which was also a concrete island, cut off by a dual carriageway and a railway. The town had many needs. During his research, Paul used a simple questionnaire and identified thirteen projects that were needed to help the town. He began with just one, a child-caring project which gave mothers more time to themselves. However, The Wire Project now has twenty initiatives and more than two hundred volunteers. That's brilliant progress!

Where do we start...?

More haste less speed. PROVERB

Be prepared. SCOUT MOTTO

There are plenty of sayings that give us advice on getting prepared. Investment in good quality community research is never wasted. It will either confirm your perceptions or throw up some big surprises.

You started with a prayer week; now is the time to do some research. As human beings we are called to love God with all our minds, as well as our hearts. That means employing our very best creative and strategic energies towards the task at hand. As we saw in Part 2 (the business and employment theme), Nehemiah was both a prayer warrior and a project manager, who diligently researched the ruined walls of Jerusalem at night with his friends. So, be prepared to do some serious research with others and be ready for that research to come up with different answers to the ones you might expect. Stay open to the God of surprises.

Even if you feel that God has called you simply to talk to the elderly people in the home across the road, it's still worth spending time on researching your community, both formally and informally. For instance, flick through any gospel and watch how Jesus spends almost as much time asking people questions as giving them answers. What a great way of building relationships! Ask questions of those you are trying to help and you'll be including and involving them in working with you to create practical solutions to the problems you face.

You'll benefit greatly from plenty of hard data to get you started, such as the size of the local population, housing, businesses, community organisations and the area's recreational facilities. Once you have your framework, a good questionnaire, some interviews and/or a focus group will give you your soft data - that's people's feelings, opinions and insights into their community.

Keep on planning and praying the whole way through. Review your results regularly in order to identify the way ahead. Even if your scheme is only small, you need to be able early on to identify the obstacles that might get in your way. There will always be some, but good planning will smooth your path considerably.

Top tips for your research and preparation

- It's important to work out a framework for your research. For example, it may be strictly geographical or among a particular group, e.g. the elderly.
- Setting realistic goals helps our faith to flourish as we see all those who are taking part in the project receive encouragement from achieving what they set out to do.
- Keep plenty of people in the loop and be prepared to amend your conclusions in the light of new information.
- Talk to your church leaders. Keep them involved and informed as you move your project forward. Don't stagnate, communicate!

It is clear from Scripture that Jesus himself had a clear understanding of his ministry and his task, and what was the right time and what wasn't. He knew when it was right to stop and talk to a woman who had touched the edge of his garment, even when he was on his way to a dying child. He knew when to withdraw to the hills to pray, when to move onto the next village, even though crowds were searching for him. He knew when to set his face resolutely towards Jerusalem, his final destination, in order to achieve a specific goal: saving grace for the whole world through his crucifixion, burial and resurrection.

Jesus knew these things because he remained close to the Father, one with him, in touch and in tune with what he was doing. Our plans, our strategy and our timing should echo God's plans for our communities. They and our research and work must be 100 per cent 'God-dependent'. As we move towards involvement, it's all the more important we remain intimate with God. Everything we do may also mean that we follow the path of sacrifice, pain and resurrection joy.

Resources

Faithworks Community Audit
This is a brilliant tool, packed full of ways to help you research your area. It includes details on how to research your community, how to gather information in the best way and how to analyse it. It includes sample questionnaires and suggests ways to move your idea forward.

Faithworks Unpacked
This is a practical manual covering planning and funding community projects as well as advice on project implementation and evaluating established projects.

STEP 3: WHAT'S IN THE CUPBOARD?
- ASSESSING YOUR RESOURCES

Small is beautiful. E. F. SCHUMACHER

Not so long ago, people would walk past the doors of a church in Edinburgh, see how dilapidated it was and assume it was closed. As it was, about ten worshippers would be there faithfully each Sunday, many of them elderly. Little did the passers-by realise that this tiny church would be the beginnings of award-winning work with bereaved children under twelve, called Richmond's Hope.

Their journey began in 1997 with the church supporting bereaved families. It became clear that the children had no one to talk to about their losses. Gradually, using people from the church and other local Christians experienced in this field, the church began to fill the gap. Small, for them, was indeed beautiful.

Assessing (or auditing) your church

Jesus said: "Suppose one of you wants to build a tower. Will he not first sit down and estimate the cost to see if he has enough money to complete it? For if he lays the foundation and is not able to finish it, everyone who sees it will ridicule him."

(Luke 14:28-29)

Begin by asking questions, such as: What space do we have? Do we have a church hall that has some rooms which are being used to store clutter? Could we borrow space from someone? Inviting someone from outside into your space can be a great way of seeing its potential through different eyes.

Assessing what your church or organisation has already got is a vital first step in planning your community project. Money, equipment, space, time, skills and ideas might be there already. But what are your weak areas? What opportunities can you spot? And is there anything which might threaten your plans? The best plans are those tailored to fit your current circumstances and meet the needs around you, in the light of the resources you have.

Don't forget your most valuable asset. Ask the question: *Who* do we have in our church? Do we have someone involved in business? Or someone who is a teacher? If you run a 24/7 Prayer room and out of it comes the seed of an idea to work in local schools, then a teacher in your congregation might be able to get you started. Alternatively, such a professional might be able to give advice or to recommend someone else for the job.

Resources

Faithworks Church Audit

This pack will help you take a fresh look at what you already have. It includes how to look at your strengths, weaknesses, opportunities and threats (a SWOT analysis) and how to use this analysis to further your vision. It also contains a ready-made set of questions to help you audit your own church.

Getting started

(Training for steps 1, 2 and 3)

'Let's go!'always sounds more attractive than 'What can our church realistically offer?' or 'What does our community really need?' But it pays to be prepared.

The Faithworks 'Getting Started' training module can help you as a local church, town-wide group of churches or as an individual with a vision. It's a one-day workshop which helps you understand your community, identify challenges and opportunities, match your community needs with what your church has got and ensure that your project is sustainable.

More information on this training and all the other training courses can be found at www.faithworks.info/training.

STEP 4: DON'T HIDE YOUR LIGHT!
- BEING DISTINCTIVELY CHRISTIAN

Always be prepared to give an answer to everyone who asks you to give the reason for the hope that you have. But do this with gentleness and respect...

(1 Peter 3:15)

Jesus once asked a rhetorical question about the wisdom of lighting a lamp and then hiding it underneath a basket. 'Don't ever be afraid to show people who you really are by your good works – let your light shine brightly in front of everyone. You are the light of the world!' (Mt. 5:14-16, paraphrased)

The people who run Gate Christian Outreach in Southampton are embodying this simple lesson. They make no secret of the fact that they are Christians as they work among prostitutes in the city. Project leader Pam Hand and fellow churchgoer Trisha Kenyon realised that the church had a unique opportunity to be a source of hope, rather than of condemnation, for the girls. 'Some people thought it was dangerous, others thought it was brave', recalls Pam. 'The important thing for us was that these girls were people with real needs.' The team of volunteers gradually got to know the girls, as they provided a weekly service of tea, coffee, friendship and prayer. With many of the women in dire straits, the volunteers found that offers of prayer were rarely declined. Through the actions of the volunteers, the prostitutes in Southampton have encountered a God who loves them and is interested in their lives.

> *Some people say debt counselling is a distraction from evangelism. But what is evangelism? It is actually being a light to the community. It means showing an alternative way of living. If you set a good example, people will want to know why.*
>
> HEATHER KEATES, Community Debt Advice Centre, Burgess Hill

One of the biggest challenges, though, is how to ensure that your project stays totally accessible to people of all backgrounds while retaining its distinctive Christian identity. The distinctive faith approach is a way of recognising and celebrating religious diversity in the UK. While accepting that there is some common ground between all of the major faith traditions, a distinctive faith approach asserts that all religious traditions are not the same and should be treated in a way that respects and affirms their differences.

Recent employment legislation actually gives a positive opportunity to Christian employers to identify and clearly articulate their distinctive Christian ethos. In order to help churches and Christian employers develop employment practices that meet the requirements of employment law, Faithworks has developed the Christian Ethos Audit Pack (see below).

> *Our motivation is simply our God-given responsibility to care – our faith must work! If through our work the people we serve encounter God and something of the love and compassion of Jesus, then that will speak for itself. We don't hide our faith, but we will never impose it. We are here to serve all, unconditionally. That is what Christ has asked us to do. It's what our faith compels us to do.*
>
> STEVE CHALKE

Resources
Faithworks Christian Ethos Audit
This helps churches and organisations think through how to define their community work with clarity about their beliefs: how their inner Christian beliefs give rise to their outer public image.

Being distinctively Christian workshop
(Training for step 4)

Faithworks can provide training to help you run community projects that are accessible and yet distinctively Christian. In today's diverse multi-faith society, your community project must be accessible to people of all backgrounds and yet still retain a distinctive Christian identity.

THE FAITHWORKS SEVEN STEP GUIDE TO ACTION

Whether you are a new, small church project or a well-established organisation, this practical workshop will help you:

- Understand and articulate your distinctive Christian identity
- Develop an ethos that ensures your community project is accessible to all
- Develop sound employment practices that reflect your ethos
- Identify and justify which posts in your organisation require Christians

More information on this training and all the other training courses can be found at www.faithworks.info/training.

STEP 5: POUNDS, PLANNING AND PENCE
– CREATE A BUSINESS PLAN AND BUDGET

A six-year-old went into a bank and asked to see the manager. She explained that her girls' club was raising money for a new clubroom and asked if he would please contribute. The banker laid a five-pound note and a penny on the desk and said, 'Take your choice, Miss.' She picked up the penny and said, 'My mother always taught me to take the smallest piece. But so I won't lose the penny, I'll wrap it up in this nice piece of paper!'

In the same way that new businesses need to present their business plan to a bank manager for a loan, new community initiatives should take an equally professional approach.

Many projects get going with the help of an initial grant. Flush with their success in obtaining an initial set-up grant, coupled with the excitement of realising their dream, the projects then forget to look to the long term. They therefore run the risk of becoming totally unsustainable. To avoid this situation developing, from the first month of business onwards thought needs to be given to recording and articulating the successes of the project, thereby demonstrating a proven track record to future potential funders.

Before setting up the Community Debt Advice Centre, in Burgess Hill, south London, Heather Keates looked around to see if there were any other churches offering models of debt advice. When she didn't find any, she looked at models provided by secular agencies and tried to draw on their good practice while discarding the bits that were unsuitable. She spent six months preparing, before opening the doors to the new project.

Creating your business plan

So the hard work is done. You've prayed, 24-7. You've got a vision. You've clarified your mission. You've worked out aims, objectives and key tasks. You've identified your key partners. You've set up a project team. You know how you're going to keep records and monitor your progress. Your financial plan is firmly in place. So what do you do next? Write it all down and turn it into a business plan...

Developing a business plan can sound tedious but can reap big rewards. The truth is that you have already done almost all the hard work and putting it into a business plan with good budgeting will place your project – as yet 'unborn' – in a position of real health and strength. Your business plan is the road map for the success of your project. It sets out the route and helps you get back on track quickly if you do stray off course. Moreover, you can use it to sell your project to potential funders.

What it needs to contain:

- Executive summary
- Introduction and mission statement
- Background and track record to date
- Analysis of needs or trends – use your research here
- Statement of aims
- Key tasks and targets – this is your action plan, with deadlines and measurable outcomes
- Management and staffing
- Financial planning – the budget with income and expenditure projections
- Immediate action plan – don't forget dates and deadlines to encourage you
- Contact details – key people involved in the project

Top tips for a good business plan:

- Keep it simple. That means short (fewer than twenty pages) and no jargon.
- Make no assumptions. Explain everything in the clearest possible way which can be understood by a fifteen-year-old who knows nothing about your plan (yes, really. It works!).
- Be bold. Use phrases that start 'We will' rather than 'We hope to.'
- Demonstrate your thought process. Use graphs and tables if necessary.
- Get someone who knows nothing about your project to proof read it and identify which parts are unclear.
- Balance overall strategy with more in-depth detail.
- Keep the plan as a living, working document. Circulate it within your church or office so people can refer to it for inspiration or to get them back on course. Make it the subject of any regular prayer meetings you may have.

Key source: *The Complete Guide to Business and Strategic Planning for Voluntary Organisations* by Alan Lawrie.

STEP 6: PAPER AND MONEY
– TOP TIPS FOR OBTAINING FUNDING

God's gifts put man's best dreams to shame.

ELIZABETH BARRETT BROWNING, *Sonnets from the Portuguese* [22]

A man there was, though some did count him mad; the more he cast away, the more he had...

JOHN BUNYAN, *The Pilgrim's Progress* [23]

Give, and it will be given to you. A good measure, pressed down, shaken together and running over, will be poured into your lap.

(Luke 6:38)

There are about 7,500 grant-making trusts and foundations in the UK, giving about £1.7 billion a year to charitable causes, including church-based community projects and other Christian community initiatives.

If you want some of that pot, get your pen out and fill in the forms! Paperwork is often an essential prerequisite to obtaining the money you need. However, don't forget to keep on praying as you pen-push, asking confidently for God's blessing and provision, both for your applications itself and for those you will be seeking to serve.

Your community project could stand or fall by the level of *regular* funding you can secure. No matter how small a project is or how large it becomes, funding is always an issue. Many projects start with good *initial* funding from a single source, but then the hard work of running the project means that the issue of future funding slips down the agenda. *Regular, ongoing funding* is an issue that must be regularly reviewed.

Historically, so-called secular funders have been reluctant to give money to faith-based organisations, so make sure that you have identified and articulated the need for your initiative very clearly and succinctly in your business plan.

Don't forget that your application should be S.M.A.R.T. if it is to stand the very best chance of success with grant-making bodies. S.M.A.R.T. means that objectives should be Specific, Measurable, Achievable, Realistic and Time-specific.

Your applications can and should communicate your passion and enthusiasm for the scheme, but try to make sure this is free of religious jargon and expressed in terms that a secular group will understand. However, it is equally important to communicate all the hard work and research that you have already put in. Don't forget to include the fruits of your research – those important bits of hard and soft data you have obtained will help supply your whole application with that winning ingredient: credibility.

Top tips for submitting your funding application(s)

- Give yourself plenty of time between when you first submit your application to when you are likely to need the funds. It will take some time to reach approval stage – or disapproval (hopefully not!).

- Try to show that you are contributing to the project regularly. This might be in terms of money, but it could also be in kind through your time, your volunteers' time, or so many hours' rental of your premises.

- It's a good idea to ask for funding over a number of years rather going for a lump sum for just one year. This will give you a breathing space and help keep your project sustainable.

- Always write and say thank you if your application is successful. Give regular updates.

- Discuss how to acknowledge the support. You may want to display the funder's logo on some of your publicity material as an expression of gratitude.

- If at first you don't succeed… don't give up! With many funders, there's always next year.

Resources for fundraising

There are plenty of places to find out where those trusts and other funds are hiding. Here are just a few:

Faithworks – publishes a monthly Funding Bulletin which provides up-to-date information on potential funders as well as fund-raising tips. Each month covers a different topic. See www.faithworks.info under resources/funding.

Access Funds – a single source for the non-profit sector to get the latest information from all funding bodies – www.access-funds.co.uk
Access Funds
PO Box 34237
London
NW5 2XU

The Association of Charitable Foundations – the website has useful advice on applying to trusts, facts and figures about UK trusts and foundations and links to websites of charitable trusts – www.acf.org.uk
ACF
Central House
14 Upper Woburn Place
London WC1H 0AE
Tel: 020 7255 4499

THE FAITHWORKS SEVEN STEP GUIDE TO ACTION

Charities Information Bureau – based in West Yorkshire, with plenty of good information – www.cibfunding.org.uk

Tel: 01924 239063

Fax: 01924 239431

The Charities Information Bureau
93 Lawefield Lane
Wakefield
West Yorkshire
WF2 8SU

The Directory of Social Change – books and training – www.dsc.org.uk

Tel: 08450 77 77 07

Funding Information – the online fundraising information resource for charities, voluntary organisations, community groups, local authorities, social enterprises and other not for profit organisations throughout the UK. Access is by subscription only. You may be able to get access through your regional/national arts board for free – www.fundinginformation.org

Registered Office:
Crane House
19 Apex Business Village
Annitsford
Northumberland
NE23 7BF

Tel: 0191 250 1969

Fax: 0191 250 2563

GrantsNet – online grant locator for UK businesses and charities – www.grantsnet.co.uk

Government Grants Website – information on grants from all major government departments – www.volcomgrants.gov.uk

National Association of Councils for Voluntary Service – links to funding and training – *www.nacvs.org.uk*

177 Arundel Street
Sheffield
S1 2NU

Tel: 0114 278 6636

Fax: 0114 278 7004

Planning and funding
(Training for steps 5 and 6)

Faithworks has developed a practical workshop, called *Grant application writing and business planning*, for anyone looking for more funding, whether a small church-based project or an established charity. The workshop will help you:

- Identify sources of funding for your community project
- Write a successful grant application
- Work out future expenditure and the income needed to run your project
- Identify sources of funding for your community project
- Present your business plan to your church, potential funders and other audiences

More information on this training and all the other training courses can be found at www.faithworks.info/training.

STEP 7: TOGETHER IS BETTER
– WORKING IN PARTNERSHIP WITH OTHERS

A community is only a community when the majority of its members are making the transition from 'the community for myself' to 'myself for the community'.

JEAN VANIER

Co-operation, not competition

ANON

Partnerships multiply impact. They strengthen each party involved. They are also a great way of developing robust ideas, which have been more fully thought through because of the diversity of the people involved. (This book is one example of a three-way partnership, one between 24-7 Prayer, Faithworks and Spring Harvest.)

The Mornington Community Project in Northern Ireland, originally initiated by an unusual collaboration between a local women's group and the Brethren-based Crescent Church, has succeeded in uniting members of both the Catholic and Protestant churches for the purpose of bringing reconciliation to the region. It now provides a coffee shop, employment training, senior citizens' groups, youth clubs and kids' clubs. This multi-faceted project straddles the divide between the two religious communities in the locality.

'We have challenged our preconceptions about who should work together,' admits project director Ken Humphries. 'Before we were able to change the way young people from different backgrounds related to each other, we had to challenge the way that local churches related to each other.'

> *After an initial feasibility study, we formed an interagency group, which included the local health visitor, a nursery nurse, a local library worker, the head of the primary school, who is the chair, and the vicar. They are mostly, though not all, Christians. It makes for a fantastic crossover of ideas. The interagency group identified early needs and still refers people to the community church, for example, for the parenting skills courses.*
>
> ROSIE DALMAN, community church worker, Keresley Village Community Church

Churches often underestimate how willing and ready other agencies and groups are to work with them. Society at large, including local and national government, is waking up to the value of long-term strategic partnerships. Platforms and opportunities exist for those who will take initiative and develop ongoing relationships with other service providers.

Perhaps you already have good working relationships with other service providers and organisations, such as your local council and local churches. But if not, seize the moment and start pushing on a few doors to partnership. Your community project can benefit greatly from developing partnerships with many other service providers, including other churches, statutory bodies and the local council.

Making the effort to forge working relationships can help your project develop a more joined-up approach and gain access to further funding opportunities. It can also be a powerful Christian witness towards those who would never step inside a church building, and it can add fuel to your prayer life – it's always easier to pray for people when you know their faces, names and problems on a personal level.

At this point, you may be wondering 'How do we make partnerships work in practice? What are the pros and cons? How can we maintain our distinctive Christian identity when working alongside government agencies and other faith groups?' This is a task that calls for ... the Faithworks Charter.

The Faithworks Charter

Faithworks has put together a charter to help people retain a distinctive Christian identity for their projects as well as being accessible to all. You'll find a full copy of it at the end of this section. The Charter is an excellent benchmark for churches and community projects to aim at as they work in the community, and has won the respect of many in both local and national government, in the media and among business people. The values embodied in the Charter make it good not just for opening doors to partnership, but also for improving our performance as churches and Christian communities, to pursue excellence in everything we do.

Resources

Customised training packages

Faithworks also provides customised training packages tailored to meet the needs of individual churches, groups of churches or Christian organisations. See www.faithworks.info/training

Faithworks Consultancy

The Faithworks Consultancy provides a range of resources, tools and services specifically tailored to assist churches and Christian projects as they seek to engage with their communities effectively and professionally. See www.faithworks.info/consultancy

Partnerships

(Training for step 7)

Faithworks offers a one-day training course entitled *How to work in partnership with other service providers.*

Whether you are a small church-based project or an established organisation, this one-day practical workshop will help you to:

- Identify opportunities and obstacles to working in partnership
- Understand the roles of other service providers and your local council
- Work effectively with other churches
- Work with secular agencies and other faith groups while maintaining your distinctive Christian identity

More information on this training and all the other training courses can be found at www.faithworks.info/training.

[22] Elizabeth Barrett Browning, *Sonnets from the Portuguese*, (W. W. Norton, 1996)

[23] John Bunyan, *The Pilgrim's Progress*, (Oxford: Oxford University Press, 2003)

JOINING THE FAITHWORKS MOVEMENT

As you take the first steps towards serving your local community, why not investigate Faithworks membership? Since its launch in 2001, Faithworks has sought to empower and inspire individual Christians, local churches and Christian projects to develop their role at the heart of their communities.

To date thousands of individuals and hundreds of churches and projects have joined Faithworks in creating a movement that is both challenging the perception of the Church and delivering real grassroots change in communities.

In essence, the Faithworks Movement exists to inspire and resource churches, Christian charities and agencies to live out their belief that faith works and to put faith back into the heart of the community.

FAITHWORKS AWARDS

Faithworks runs an annual awards programme which provides funds and strategic support for carefully selected Christian projects serving their local communities. The awards are a celebration of the success of the thousands of innovative, church-based social action projects and organisations around the country.

For more details on the current scheme, see www.faithworks.info/awards05

FAITHWORKS CONFERENCE

Faithworks also organises a biennial conference with internationally renowned speakers. The next one runs from 4th-6th November 2005 in Eastbourne.

Faithworks believes that the church has a key role to play in building public trust in society. This conference will be a forum to talk about how that can be achieved, with input from Tony Campolo, Steve Chalke, Geraldine Latty, Jeff Lucas, Nims Obunge, Cardinal Cormac Murphy-O'Connor, Jim Wallis and others.

Find out more information about the Faithworks Conference at: www.faithworks.info/conference.

FAITHWORKS MEMBERSHIP

Membership is free and you will join the 17,000 and growing number of people who have signed up to wanting to make a difference. At the heart of the Faithworks Movement are its members. As a member you will be joining with one voice to say that faith works. You will be helping us to:

- Create a mandate for change, as we endeavour to engage on your behalf with both government and media at a national level.
- Tackle the negative media coverage of the church and tell the story once again of faith in action, transforming lives and communities.

FAITHWORKS AFFILIATION

Alternatively, you may want to affiliate your church, organisation or community project to Faithworks. Sign the Faithworks Charter, pay the £20 affiliation fee and you will be able to access the many benefits of affiliation, which include free downloads of audit packs and discounts on all Faithworks training and events.

FAITHWORKS LOCAL NETWORKS

A Faithworks Local Network provides a way for individual Christians and churches to explore ways of developing social action projects in their locality together. It could also be a means of connecting existing social action projects being delivered across a town or a wider area. Alternatively it may take the form of a charity that unites several churches for the purposes of service delivery

Obviously each network must be appropriate to its local context; however, all Faithworks Local Networks share a commitment to working towards the standards of best practice set out in the Faithworks Charter.

The benefits of forming a faithworks Local Charter are:
- Churches can achieve far more in their local community by working together than they can by working alone – this has been Faithworks' experience..
- Networks are more effective than individual churches when seeking to liaise with and release resources from local authorities.
- A customised logo along with permission to use the name of Faithworks in your branding.
- Discounts on bulk orders of Faithworks books and resources for churches or individuals that are part of your local network.
- Opportunities to host regional Faithworks training events in order to equip network members at discounted rates.
- A dedicated web page at www.faithworks.info to publish membership contact details and information about the work of your local network.

Contact us:

If you would like any more information or assistance concerning Faithworks, please don't hesitate to contact us at:

Faithworks, 115 Southwark Bridge Road, London, SE1 0AX

020 7450 9031   info@faithworks.info

Ruth Liley

THE FAITHWORKS CHARTER

- *Principles for churches and local Christian agencies committed to excellence in community work and service provision in the UK*
- *A corporate commitment to use during your commissioning service/event at the finale of your prayer week (see end of Part 2 of this book)*
- *You are welcome to make photocopies of the Faithworks Charter (below) to give to people:*

Motivated by our Christian faith we _____

commit ourselves to the following standards as we serve others in our community work and seek to model trust.

Signed_____ Date _____

Position_____

We will provide an inclusive service to our community by:

1 Serving and respecting all people regardless of their gender, marital status, race, ethnic origin, religion, age, sexual orientation or physical and mental capability.

2 Acknowledging the freedom of people of all faiths or none both to hold and to express their beliefs and convictions respectfully and freely, within the limits of the UK law.

3 Never imposing our Christian faith or belief on others.

4 Developing partnerships with other churches, voluntary groups, statutory agencies and local government wherever appropriate in order to create an effective, integrated service for our clients avoiding unnecessary duplication of resources.

5 Providing and publicising regular consultation and reporting forums to client groups and the wider community regarding the effective development and delivery of our work and our responsiveness to their actual needs.

We will value all individuals in a way that is consistent with our distinctive Christian ethos by:

1 Creating an environment where clients, volunteers and employees are encouraged and enabled to realise their potential.

2 Assisting our clients, volunteers and employees to take responsibility for their own learning and development, both through formal and informal training opportunities and ongoing assessment.

3 Developing an organisational culture in which individuals learn from any mistakes made and where excellence and innovation are encouraged and rewarded.

4 Promoting the value of a balanced, holistic lifestyle as part of each individual's overall personal development.

5 Abiding by the requirements of employment law in the UK and implementing best employment practices and procedures designed to maintain our distinctive ethos and values.

We will develop a professional approach to management, practice and funding by:

1 Implementing a management structure, which fosters and encourages participation by staff at all levels in order to facilitate the fulfilment of the project's goals and visions.

2 Setting and reviewing measurable and timed outcomes annually, and regularly to evaluate and monitor our management structure and output, recognising the need for ongoing organisational flexibility, development and good stewardship of resources.

3 Doing all we can to ensure that we are not over-dependent on any one source of funding.

4 Implementing best practice procedures in terms of Health and Safety and Child Protection in order to protect our staff, volunteers and clients.

5 Handling our funding in a transparent and accountable way and to give relevant people from outside our organisation/project reasonable access to our accounts.

RESOURCES SECTION

BOOKS FROM PART 1

24-7 Prayer, The 24-7 Prayer Manual, (Eastbourne: Kingsway, 2003)
Coupland, D., *Life After God*, (London: Scribner,1994)
Greig, P. & Roberts, D., *Red Moon Rising*, (Eastbourne: Kingsway, 2003)
Greig, P., *Vision and Vow*, (Eastbourne: Kingsway, 2005)
Heasley, B. & Jobe, B., *Writing on the Wall*, (forthcoming)
Honoré, C., *In Praise of Slow*, (London: Orion, 2004)
Middleton, J.R. & Walsh, B.J., *Truth is Stranger than it used to be*, (London: SPCK,1995)

BOOKS FROM PART 2

Family

Campbell, R., *How to Really Love Your Teenager*, (Carlisle: Authentic Media, 1999)
Chalke, S., *How to Succeed as a Parent*, (London: Hodder & Stoughton, 1997)
Chalke, S., *How to Succeed as a Working Parent*, (London: Hodder & Stoughton, 2003)
Clapp, R., *Families at the Crossroads*, (Leicester: IVP, 1993)
Ash, C., *Marriage: Sex in the Service of God*, (Leicester: IVP, 2003)
Van Leeuwen, M., *Fathers and Sons*, (Leicester: IVP, 2002)
Robinson, J., *Nobody's Child: The Stirring True Story of an Unwanted Boy Who Found Hope*, (Oxford: Monarch Publications, 2003)
Sheppard, L., *Boys Becoming Men*, (Carlisle: Authentic/Spring Harvest Publishing Division, 2002)
Storkey, E., *The Search for Intimacy*, (London: Hodder and Stoughton,1996)
Tufnell, C. and Worth, J., *All Alone – Help and Hope for Single Parents*, (Carlisle: Authentic/Spring Harvest Publishing Division, 2002)

Business and employment

Greene, M., *Thank God it's Monday*, (Bletchley: Scripture Union, 2001)
Greene, M., *Pocket Prayers for Work*, (London: Church House Publishing, 2004)
Rendle, S. and Steffen, T., *Great Commission Companies,* (Downers Grove: IVP, 2003)
Toynbee, P., *Hard Work,* (London: Bloomsbury, 2003)
Klein, N., *No Logo,* (London: Flamingo, 2000)
Sherman, D. and Hendricks, W., *Your Work Matters to God,* (Colorado: Navpress, 1987)
Hood, N., *God's Payroll: Whose Work Is It Anyway?,* (Carlisle: Authentic, 2003)
Lawrie, A., *The Complete Guide to Business and Strategic Planning,* (2nd edn), (London: Directory of Social Change, 2001)

Politics, law and order

Aitken, J., *Pride and Perjury*, (London: Continuum, 2003)
Bartley, J., *The Subversive Manifesto*, (Oxford: BRF, 2003)

Chalke, S., and Watkis, A., *Trust: A Radical Manifesto,* (Milton Keynes: Authentic/Spring Harvest publishing division, 2004)

Haugen, G. A., *Good News about Injustice*, (Leicester: IVP, 2002)

McIlroy, D., *Christian Perspectives on Law – a Biblical View of Law and Justice*, (Milton Keynes: Paternoster Press, 2004)

Paxman, J., *Friends in High Places* (London: Penguin, 1991)

Paxman, J., *The Political Animal*, (London: Penguin, 2003)

Sampson, A., *Who Runs this Place?*, (London: John Murray, 2005)

Spencer, N., *Votewise*, (London: SPCK, 2004)

Wallis, J., *God's Politics: Why the Right Gets It Wrong and the Left Doesn't Get It*, (HarperSanFrancisco, 2005)

The excluded

Apichella, M., *The Church's Hidden Asset – Empowering the Older Generation*, (Stowmarket: Kevin Mayhew, 2001)

Spencer, N., *Asylum and Immigration*, (Milton Keynes: Paternoster Press, 2004)

Swithinbank, T., *Coming Up from the Streets – The story of the Big Issue*, (Earthscan, 2001)

BOOKS FROM PART 3:

Chalke, S., *Faithworks: Unpacked*, (Eastbourne: Kingsway, 2002)

Chalke, S. & Jackson, T., *Faithworks: Stories of Hope*, (Eastbourne: Kingsway, 2001)

Chalke, S. & Johnston, S., *Faithworks: Intimacy & Involvement*, (Eastbourne: Kingsway, 2003)

Chalke, S. & Watkis, A., *100 Proven Ways to Transform Your Community*, (Eastbourne: Kingsway, 2003)

Chalke, S. & Watkis, A., *Trust: A Radical Manifesto*, (Milton Keynes: Authentic/Spring Harvest publishing division, 2004)

Faithworks Church Audit (London: Faithworks, 2002)

Faithworks Community Audit (London: Faithworks, 2002)

Faithworks Christian Ethos Audit (London: Faithworks, 2003)

JOURNALS

John Wesley's Journal

VIDEOS

Faithworks Different video (£5)

Different is a teaching video divided into four sessions and is ideal for small groups, including leadership teams. It helps those of us who are looking for ways to integrate faith with local community involvement. It examines the radical and inclusive message of Jesus, and the challenge of being authentically Christian: in, but not of, the world.

WEBSITES

www.24-7prayer.com
www.24-7mission.com
www.boiler-rooms.com
www.faithworks.info